Sam Stern's

eat

vegetarian

with Susan Stern

WALKER BOOKS

CONTENTS

Welcome to my new book – a collection of my favourite vegetarian recipes all mixed up with some tasty new ones. Veggie food is up there with the best. So whether you're a committed vegetarian or just like eating good food that happens to be meat-free, you'll find loads in here to get cooking. Added bonus? Vegetarian food is some of the healthiest around so you can feel good about yourself as you're enjoying it. It's also pretty kind to the pocket, which is never a bad thing. If you're cooking for yourself, your family or mates, there's food here to take you through from breakfast to dinner. So dive in and have yourself a great time.

EAT VEGETARIAN

Do it with style. Choose the right food and cook it brilliantly – never compromising on quality or flavour. But whatever your reasons for going veggie (ethics – animal rights, green issues – cost or health) there are rules. Giving up meat and fish is a big step. So check what you need to be eating to keep fit and healthy. If you're a first time veggie why not take a couple of days to try it out? Maybe put a few meals together with a mate or your family. If you're eating a mixed diet and just want to expand your veggie repertoire, check the facts anyway – it's always interesting.

WHAT'S OUT – meat, fish, shellfish and animal by-products, e.g. gelatine, rennet, fat, whey, some emulsifiers.

WHAT'S IN – fruit, vegetables, dairy products, soy products, pulses, grains, nuts, seeds, eggs, salad. Doesn't seem like a lot but break each section down and you've got hundreds of ingredients for creative cooking.

WHAT WORKS AND WHY – variety's the key. Just eating chips and egg or plates of salad won't do it. For a balanced diet that's as healthy as that of most meat eaters, you need to do four things.

1. Eat a range of foods across the 5 basic food groups. Every food has a unique nutritional make-up so spreading the pleasure means you get the best diet.
2. Veggie protein isn't complete so get the full range of essential amino acids by combining food groups, e.g. Beans on Toast; Rice & Veggie Chilli; Tomato & Lentil Soup & a Cheese Fat Rascal.
3. It can be harder to get calcium, iron, vitamin B12 and selenium in a purely veggie or vegan diet. Double check you're getting enough.

4. Use the chart opposite as the basis for your cooking but don't go obsessively carving up every single meal into nutritional categories – it'll ruin the eating. Spread the load across the day. Though specially watch what you're doing when demanding stuff comes up – exams, half-marathon, wall-to-wall partying. Hey, once you know what you're doing, it gets to be instinctive.

THE STRATEGY

Shopping for veggie foods is all about getting the freshest fruit and veg possible (they lose texture, taste and nutrients with age) and reading labels.

WHAT TO GET
* Check the chart opposite and storecupboard basics (pg 9).
* Don't buy too much – you'll chuck it away.
* Buy bargains (oil, multi-pack beans, pasta etc).

FOOD GROUP	WHY YOU NEED IT	WHERE TO GET IT	HOW MUCH
Carbs	Energy (sport, thought, movement, survival) building bone/cartilage/nerves, general body maintenance.	Spuds, root veg, breads, grains, whole grain cereal, pasta, rice, pulses, noodles, fruit, oats, lentils, fruit, dried fruit, some dairy (yogurt/ creamy cheeses, milk), nuts, seeds, mushrooms.	At least 5 portions a day – a third of your daily diet
Fruit and vegetables	Disease prevention, immune system boosting, good for hair, skin, bone strength for sport. Packed with vital vitamins, minerals, fibre for energy, plus calcium, zinc, potassium, which can be low in a veggie diet.	Every fruit and vegetable has particular nutrients so eat a variety. Darker-skinned varieties of both, and darker-leaved veg are more nutritious. So mix colours and varieties to keep the cooking interesting and the nutrients varied. Juices count, as do frozen and canned.	At least 3 fruit and 3 veg per day but as many as you fancy
Milk and dairy (calcium)	Strengthens bones and teeth – you need them. Dairy is brilliant for essential calcium plus protein and minerals. Missing out on calcium leads to osteoporosis – vegans need to find substitutes.	All cheeses, yogurts, milk, soy milk. Also find calcium in soy beans, leafy green veg, sesame seeds, tahini, almonds, tofu, bread, oats, watercress, dried apricots, figs, brazil nuts, pinenuts, pistachios, pecans – crucial for vegans and non-dairy eaters.	2–3 portions daily
Protein	Growth, muscle repair, metabolism. Essential for growing and maintaining health. You can't store it so eat some daily. Combine incomplete veggie proteins with another food group to make them active – see opposite.	Complete protein found in quinoa, egg whites, soy beans, soy protein. Incomplete protein in dried/tinned beans, chickpeas, peas, lentils, tofu, nuts, seeds, couscous, bulgur wheat, wholegrains, cereal, eggs, baked beans, yogurt, hummus, milk, cheese, broccoli, beansprouts, peas, seaweed (nori), sweet potato, dried apricots, avocado, miso.	2 portions daily
Fat	Essential for maintaining the body's processes – energy, activating vitamins, insulation.	Butter, vegetable spread and soy milk/spread/ oils. Cheese, cream – but not too much. Olive, rapeseed, sunflower oils. Avocado.	2 portions daily
Iron	Low-iron diets can cause anaemia (it's hard to focus, you feel and look flaky, no energy) particularly in girls. All veggies are susceptible. Iron needs to be eaten with Vitamin C so the body can absorb it e.g. oranges/juice, kiwi, strawberry, potato, cabbage, broccoli, tomato, melon, asparagus, peppers, mango, blackberries.	Nuts, seeds, figs, raisins, eggs, spinach, kidney beans, chickpeas, black treacle, lentils, peanut butter, hummus, wholemeal flour, watercress, broccoli, spring greens, okra, spinach, bread, olives.	Daily
Selenium	Vulnerability to colds etc if you don't get some of this – it's essential for the immune system.	Nuts – brazils are good. Two a day would do it. Wholemeal bread and eggs, brown rice.	Daily
Vitamin B12	Can be low in veggies and particularly vegans – needed for nervous system and to keep blood healthy (fights anaemia).	Eggs, dairy products, Vegemite, Marmite, soy milks, veg & sunflower spreads.	Daily

* Living with carnivores? Share basics – rice etc.
* Don't shop when hungry – you'll snack out.
* Write a list – plan ahead for meals and stick to it.
* Factor in use of left-overs – saves time/energy.
* Plan to cook more than you need, and freeze.
* Cook veggie lunches to go.
* Shop yourself so you can read the labels.

WHERE TO SHOP
* Health food shops cater for veggie and vegan specialities and fair trade.
* Ethnic shops do a range of exotic spices, herbs, grains, pulses, fruit and vegetables, and are great value.
* Farmers, local greengrocers and markets are best for value and freshness and what's in season.
* Supermarkets do a good range of veggie foods.

READ THE LABELS
* Always do it to know what you're getting.
* Know what to look for – some things are hidden.
* Trust the Vegetarian Society symbol (V).
* Where does it come from? Look for food miles.
* Check sell-by dates – find the freshest.

WATCH FOR HIDDEN INGREDIENTS
* Gelatine – in jellies, some jam, yogurt, mayo, dressings, spreads, sauces, sweets.
* Animal fat (lard, suet) – used in many pastries, breads, biscuits, cakes.
* Rennet – in cheeses. Look for vegetable rennet.
* Whey – usually created using animal rennet. In some muesli, bread, chocolate, crisps.
* Shrimp paste – in some curry pastes/sauces.
FOR VEGANS
* Avoid albumen, lactose, honey and use egg replacer.
* Check Vegan Society website for info.

GROW YOUR OWN
* Grow own parsley, coriander, basil, chillies in pots on windowsill or in garden.
* Grow spuds in old tyres.
* Get an allotment – join a community garden.
* Grow eggs – get chickens.

STORE IT PROPERLY
* Wrap herbs, beansprouts in kitchen roll/plastic bag in chiller of fridge.
* Wrap cheese in paper, store in box in chiller of fridge.
* Store tomatoes and strawberries at room temperature.
* Store bananas separately from other fruit; they over-ripen.
* Wrap hard tomatoes/avocados in paper to ripen.
* Eggs in the fridge? Get to room temp for baking.
* Freeze own pizza bases, stuffed baked spuds, pancakes, loaf cakes, pies, stews, hummus, curries, cooked beans, loaves, sliced bread.
* Living with carnivores? Put their meat/fish on the bottom shelf.

BEFORE YOU COOK
* Read the recipe through.
* Check you've got the ingredients (or substitutes).
* Sort out timings and equipment.
* Line tins and pre-heat the oven if needed.
* Wash fruit and veg properly in cold water.
* Nutrients sit near the skin, so if you can cook without peeling, do.
* Wash salad leaves gently. Blot dry or spin.
* Save vegetable trimmings for stock.
* Fruit and veg lose nutrients once chopped – so don't do it too soon.
* Save energy – boil the kettle then pour into pan.
* Use the right size pan.
* Don't preheat the oven too soon.
* Cooking with carnivores – keep your stuff separate.

THE VEGGIE STORECUPBOARD

Loads of these ingredients last for ages – so you've got the means for great meals already in your cupboard. Freeze frozen fruit and veg, and left-overs.

PULSES
Beans: kidney, soya, haricot, cannellini, blackeye, black, butter, adzuki, pinto, borlotti, broad bean, flageolet, mung (for sprouting), re-fried beans, baked beans
Lentils: red, Puy, green, brown
Chickpeas

GRAINS
Rice: brown, long grain, basmati, jasmine sticky, risotto (Arborio/Vialone Nano)
Oats: porridge, flaked
Couscous
Polenta
Bulgur wheat
Quinoa

PASTAS
Dried or fresh spaghetti, linguine, tagliatelle, penne, lasagne, cannelloni etc.
Noodles: egg or rice

EGGS
Free-range or egg replacer (vegan)

MEAT SUBSTITUTE
Tofu
Quorn

DAIRY
Any veggie cheese: e.g. Cheddar/Gruyère/feta/halloumi/veggie Parmesan
Crème fraîche, sour cream,
whipping cream
Semi-skimmed milk
Soy, rice, almond milk (vegan)
Butter
Soya/olive/vegetable/sunflower spread (vegan)

OILS
Olive oil (cooking)
Extra-virgin (dressings)
Groundnut (curries, stir-fry)
Sesame (stir-fry)
Sunflower, rapeseed (frying, roasting)

STOCK
Marigold Swiss Bouillon

VINEGARS
Malt, rice, red/white wine, cider, balsamic

CONDIMENTS
Tomato ketchup
Mushroom ketchup
Henderson's Relish
Harissa paste
Curry paste
Chilli jam
Branston pickle
Soy sauce
Sweet chilli sauce
Hoisin sauce
Teriyaki sauce
HP Sauce
Mayonnaise (vegan mayo)
Chinese cooking wine
Tabasco

ESSENTIAL CANS/JARS
Tomatoes: plum, chopped
Tomato purée
Passata, creamed tomatoes
Sweetcorn
Capers
Olives
Dill pickles
Jalapeño peppers

SPICES & SEASONINGS
Sea salt, fine salt
Black peppercorns
Chinese 5 spice
Curry powder
Ground cinnamon
Turmeric
Cumin (ground and seeds)
Onion seeds (nigella)
Garam masala
Coriander (ground and seeds)
Cardamom pods
Fennel seeds
Paprika (plain, smoked, sweet)
Chilli: powder, flakes
Cinnamon: ground, sticks
Ground ginger
Nutmeg
Mixed spice
Vanilla: extract, pods
Dried oregano, basil, rosemary, dill
Tubes/jars of lazy lemongrass, ginger, garlic, coriander
Fresh limes/lemons, or bottled
Fresh garlic
Fresh chillies
Shallots/onions

DRIED FRUIT
Apricots, figs, cranberries, sour cherries
Raisins, sultanas, dates, currants

NUTS
Brazils, hazelnuts, walnuts, cashews, pecans, peanuts, almonds, pistachios, chestnuts (tin or vacpack)

SEEDS
Sesame, pumpkin, poppy, sunflower

FLOURS
White: plain, self-raising
Wholemeal: plain, self-raising
Gram (chickpea)
Cornflour
Baking Powder
Bicarbonate of Soda

SWEETENERS
Honey, golden syrup, maple syrup, black treacle, soft brown sugar, granulated sugar, caster sugar, icing sugar, chocolate

SPREADS
Peanut butter, jam, lemon curd, Marmite, Vegemite

STAPLES
Keep a store of onions and potatoes

THE COOKING

There's no need for special equipment but a steamer's useful and a couple of sharp knives for chopping veg. Segregate your chopping boards if cooking with carnivores. A wok is good, and a handblender. Get these basic techniques down and enjoy yourself.

SIFT
Give flour/other dry ingredients a good shake through a sieve to aerate, mix, smooth and lighten.

RUB IN
Incorporate flour and fat by rubbing lightly between fingertips till mix looks like fine breadcrumbs – hold hands high over bowl to aerate.

CREAM
Mix soft butter and sugar to a light airy cream by beating for 5 minutes with a wooden spoon in a warm bowl using brisk wrist action.

FOLD IN
Incorporate ingredients like flour, melted chocolate, whisked egg whites into any mix by using a large metal spoon and gentle figure-of-8 scooping movements.

BEAT
Blend ingredients together using a wooden spoon/balloon whisk/fork and v strong wrist action (use for eggs, batters, cakes, sauces, etc).

BLITZ
Blend or fragment food with handblender/processor/blender (use for soups, smoothies, dips, breadcrumbs).

SIMMER
Cook food or liquid at just below boiling point (it sounds and looks calm, bubbles sometimes, and cooks steadily without burning/toughening).

SEASON
Add salt, pepper to boost flavour. Also use lemon/lime juice, spices, garlic, ginger, onions, mushroom ketchup, vinegars, fresh/dried herbs.

MARINATE
Sit fruit/veg/tofu/Quorn/cheese in mix of oils, herbs, yogurt, garlic, sauces, seasoning. Leave a while to flavour.

CHOP
Cut food into different sizes as specified in recipe using a small sharp knife on a flat surface.
Dice: small or tiny regular cubes.
Finely chop: very small bits.
Slice: cut across.
Roughly chop: go freestyle.
Bite-size: bite-size bits.
Shred: cut veg across in thin ribbons.

THE HOW TO

SEPARATE EGGS

Tap egg sharply on side of bowl to crack the middle. Hold over bowl and open it with both thumbs, tilting to one side so yolk ends up in one half of shell. Let white spill into bowl. Tip yolk/rest of white into empty half of shell, spilling more white. Repeat. Tip separated yolk into second bowl.

WHISK EGG WHITES

Check whites are totally yolk-free (or they won't work) and utensils, hands, bowls are grease-free. Whisk in a large bowl with balloon, electric or handwhisk. Whisk slowly at first, then faster for soft peaks. Continue for stiff peaks. Don't overbeat – loses air.

KNEAD DOUGH

Roll dough into a ball on floured board/surface. Press down and away with heel of your hand. Fold dough back over. Turn. Repeat for 8–10 minutes, roughing up and stretching it till smooth/elastic.

CHOP AN ONION

Top and tail onion with small sharp knife on board. Peel off papery then brown skin. Sit onion upright. Hold firmly. Cut down into thin slices, stopping 1cm/¼ in before the base to hold it together. Gripping firmly, turn it onto its side. Slice down and through. It will fall into small dice.

STOP ONIONS BURNING

Add a tiny pinch of salt to onions in the pan. Modify heat.

STOP BUTTER BURNING

Add a little oil to the pan with the butter. Modify heat.

ROLL OUT PASTRY AND GET IT INTO A TIN

Sit ball of pastry on a lightly floured surface next to greased tin to judge size required to cover base and sides. Roll pastry out lightly using floured rolling pin. Turn a few times until you get the size, shape and thickness required. Lift it into the tin – for larger bits, roll pin underneath and lift across. Fit into corners/sides and mould. Trim. Keep any spare for repairs in case pastry shrinks in cooking. Mould into cracks. Cook a further 3–4 minutes.

MAKE CROÛTONS

Preheat oven to 200°C/400°F/gas 6. Chop 2–3 slices of white bread/baguette/ciabatta and roll in a mix of a cut clove of garlic in a little oil. Bake on a tray in oven for 8 minutes or till crisp. They burn fast.

PREP TOFU

Unwrap firm tofu. Sit between two chopping boards. Put weights on top for 30 minutes to press out excess water. Drain well.

MELT CHOCOLATE

Break bits into heatproof bowl. Sit it into open top of a pan of barely simmering water. Check base isn't touching water and liquid/steam can't get into chocolate. Let it melt slowly without stirring. Remove bowl from pan. Stir choc and use in recipe.

MAKE DRY/FRESH BREADCRUMBS

Leave bread out for hours, uncovered until crisp/dry. Blitz/grate to fine crumbs. Fresh? Blitz bread.

COOK PASTA

Allow 110g/4oz per person. Boil up loads of water in a large pot. Add 1 tsp salt. Add pasta. Stir once. Time once re-boiling. Boil 3–4 minutes for fresh – see pack for dried. Test before due. Eat al dente (with a bit of bite) or softer if you prefer. Drain.

COOK RICE

Allow 50g/2oz per person. For long-grain (white), e.g. basmati: rinse in cold water. Add to pan of boiling water. Reduce heat. Simmer undisturbed for 10 minutes till plump/soft (test it). Drain. Cover. Fluff with a fork after 3 minutes.

For brown: as above but cook for up to 30 minutes.

For Thai sticky: as above, but don't rinse it and don't fluff it. Safety alert: cold rice gets toxic fast. For salads, left-overs, cool on tray. Chill immediately. Eat within 2 days.

COOK DRIED BEANS

Weigh beans (50g/2oz dried beans/chickpeas per person or as recipe). Wash. Soak for 12 hours or overnight in a bowl covered with three times volume of cold water. Drain. Heat in a pan covered with fresh cold water and a pinch of bicarb to soften skins. Boil vigorously for 10 minutes (vital for red kidney beans to destroy toxins. Boil soya beans for 1 hour.) Reduce heat slightly, boiling for 45–60 minutes/until cooked through (could take much longer. Soya take 3–4 hours.) Don't add salt (it toughens beans). Drain. Freeze extras.

COOK LENTILS

Wash and remove stones/bits. Boil vigorously in loads of (already boiling) water for first 5 minutes to help digestion. Total cooking times: brown lentils – 25–30 minutes; green – 15–20 minutes; Puy – add to cold water, boil, cook 10–15 minutes; red and yellow – as recipe.

COOK BULGUR

Pour 600ml/1 pint boiling water over 110g/4oz bulgur wheat. Leave, covered, 15–30 minutes till soft. Drain well. Spread to dry or squeeze in tea towel. Fork to fluff it.

COOK QUINOA

Allow 50g/2oz per person. Rinse well. Simmer 10 minutes in twice volume of water on low heat. The grain and seed separate when cooked. Remove. Cover till water absorbed.

BOIL AN EGG

Boil a small pan of water. Add a pinch of salt. Lower egg in on a spoon. Set timer when water re-boils: 4 minutes for soft-boiled; 5 minutes for medium; 6 minutes if straight from fridge; 8 minutes for hard-boiled. Cool under cold water.

HOW TO USE THIS BOOK

Follow the signs…

 FEEDS 1 how many it feeds

 VEGAN vegan

 VEGAN OPT. vegan option: substitute dairy/eggs with vegan produce

 EXPRESS fast to cook

MEASURING: don't stress about getting ingredients exact unless baking/pastry-making.

SEASONING: use to boost flavours.

PLATING UP: make everything look great.

TEAMING: experiment with different menu combos.

PANICKING: don't. If something goes wrong, start again.

SURPRISE: every time you make a dish it tastes/looks different.

ECONOMY: save waste, energy wherever you can – go green.

SPEEDY BREAKFAST
& BRUNCH

SMOOTHIES

Sort yourself any one of these for breakfast. They're all easy and brilliant for you.
No time to drink it here and now? Bottle it up and take it with you.

Wake-up Strawberry

A sweet way to start the day and a great vitamin C boost.

1–2 bananas
Good handful strawberries
Runny honey to taste
225ml/8fl oz chilled milk/soy milk
Bit of natural/vanilla yogurt (pg 18) (optional)

1. Slice or break bananas. Chop strawberries if large.
2. Tip into blender or tall plastic jug for hand blending.
3. Add honey, milk, optional yogurt.
4. Blitz or blend.
5. Taste, adjust if you need to and re-blend.

YOU CAN

* blitz in 2 tbsps muesli, more liquid
* add blueberries or blackberries

Pineapple Punch

Fresh has the edge but tinned works in this fizzy smoothie.

¼ fresh pineapple, peeled cut into chunks
1–2 bananas
125ml/4fl oz orange juice
3–4 ice cubes
Tiny pinch salt
Squeeze lemon juice (optional)

1. Tip chunks of pineapple into a blender or jug with remaining ingredients.
2. Blitz or blend till light and fluffy.

YOU CAN

* add fresh mint
* add milk/yogurt/honey for creamy option

Mango Smooth

Creamy, rich – a bit like a lassi.

1 ripe mango, peeled
125ml/4fl oz milk/soy milk
150ml/5fl oz natural yogurt
2 tsps runny honey/caster sugar
Pinch salt
Water if needed

1. Slice mango or chop small.
2. Tip into blender/jug with other ingredients. Blitz or blend.
3. Thin with water if needed.

YOU CAN

* add banana, raspberries, fresh or tinned pineapple
* squeeze in orange/lime juice
* enjoy with a curry

Raspberry Special

Taste of childhood in a healthy glassful.

175g/6oz raspberries
1 banana
180ml/6fl oz orange juice
125ml/4fl oz natural or vanilla yogurt
Drizzle runny honey
2 ice cubes

1. Tip everything into a blender or jug.
2. Blitz or blend till smooth.

YOU CAN

* add vanilla extract
* freeze for ice-cream

Blueberry Cool

Brain boosting pre-exam soother and superfood boost. Plenty of useful antioxidants.

Handful of blueberries
1 banana, sliced
2 scoops of vanilla yogurt, or 2 tbsps of vanilla ice-cream
125ml/4fl oz milk/soy

1. Blitz everything together.

YOU CAN

* add a handful of raspberries

Simple Banana

Basic but brilliant first thing or before a big night out – enjoy after training.

1–2 ripe bananas, sliced
Drizzle runny honey
A few drops vanilla extract
(optional)
225ml/8fl oz chilled milk/yogurt

Blend or blitz everything in a jug with handblender.

YOU CAN

* sprinkle with cinnamon, grated chocolate
* add a juiced fresh orange
* add half a juiced lemon
* add 1 tbsp peanut butter
* add 2 tbsps muesli

Watermelon Cocktail

Light, refreshing and tasty – high in nutrients.

1 large slice chilled watermelon
4–6 large strawberries
Juice of 1 lemon
125ml/4fl oz apple juice

1. Remove pips and rind from watermelon.
2. Cut into chunks.
3. Remove stalks from strawberries.
4. Tip fruit into blender/jug with lemon and apple juices.
5. Blitz or blend. Add optionals. Blend again. Serve as is or with ice.

YOU CAN

* freeze smoothie mix for healthy ice cream or lollies
* thaw frozen smoothie mix overnight. Blitz or blend next morning.
* frozen fruit gives a thicker, cooler mix so keep a load in the freezer
* pick your own fruit or buy in season. Freeze to use in winter.
* lactose intolerant? Use non-dairy alternatives (soy, rice milk, fruit juice)
* add protein powder to smoothies for extra nutrient
* add bran or blitzed bran sticks for extra fibre

YOU CAN

* add a bit of grated ginger
* blitz watermelon, grated ginger and ice together for a slushie

Winter-fruit Smoothie

Packed with iron, energy and everyday essentials.

1–2 tbsps dried fruit salad (pg 37)
1 banana, sliced
225ml/8fl oz milk/soy milk
1–2 tbsps muesli (pg 20)

1. Remove any stones from fruit.
2. Tip into blender or jug with banana.
3. Add milk. Blitz. Add muesli. Blitz.
4. Add more milk if needed.
5. Blitz or blend. Serve as is or with ice.

Strawberry OJ

Perfect slushie-style in summer.

2 bananas, sliced, frozen
2–3 handfuls strawberries
225ml/8fl oz orange juice
(carton or fresh)

1. Tip fruit into blender/jug.
2. Add juice. Blend or blitz with handblender.
3. Taste. Thin with water if needed.

YOU CAN

* freeze in ice-lolly moulds for later

Peach Sherbet

Just peachy ... non-dairy.

1 large ripe peach/nectarine, chopped
1 banana
Handful strawberries/raspberries
Drizzle runny honey
125ml/4fl oz apple/orange juice
A little lemon or lime juice

1. Slice fruit. Freeze on baking paper on tin. Tip into blender or plastic jug.
2. Blitz with honey and fruit juice. Taste. Add lemon/lime juice.

YOU CAN

* use apricots for added iron

YOGURT

Its distinctive taste and texture beats yogurt you can buy. Stir in honey, sugar, syrup, jam – add wholegrain cereal or any fruit – for a cheap and healthy speedy breakfast.

MAKES 1 LITRE

1 litre/1¾ pints semi-skimmed/ whole milk
3 tbsps live natural yogurt

Brilliant Own-style Yogurt

1. Boil milk in a deep pan. Remove from heat as it rises.

2. Tip into bowl. Leave. Stir in yogurt when milk is lukewarm. Cover with clingfilm. Leave in warm place 6–8 hours or till it thickens. Wrap a towel round the bowl if it's chilly.

3. Keep covered in fridge. Eat. Save 3 tbsps for making next batch.

YOU CAN
✱ go Greek: strain yogurt through muslin till it's as thick as you like it
✱ use for smoothies, tzatziki (pg 53), raita (pg 57), salad dressings, cream cheese (pg 187) and breakfast bowls
✱ make and store it in a wide-necked flask

Banana Boost
Packed with potassium and energy.

1–2 ripe bananas
Natural yogurt
Drizzle honey
Walnuts/seeds/dried dates

1. Mash or slice bananas.
2. Mix with yogurt and honey.
3. Top with nuts/seeds/dates and more honey.

YOU CAN

* skip the nuts/seeds, add grated chocolate

Lemon Cheesecake
Tastes like the real thing...

1–2 digestive biscuits, crumbled
4 heaped tbsps Greek yogurt
2–3 tbsps cream cheese (pg 187)
A little lemon zest
1 tsp lemon juice
1 tsp honey

1. Crumble biscuits into the base of a bowl.

2. Mix other ingredients till smooth.
3. Taste and adjust to get the balance right. Pour over base.
4. Top with honey, jam or fruit sauce (pg 183), feather with a cocktail stick.

YOU CAN

* stir lemon curd (pg 187) into yogurt

Yorkshire Rhubarb
Layered-up vitamin C fest.

1 small orange
3–4 tbsps cooked rhubarb (pg 173)
Natural yogurt
A few hazelnuts, chopped
Honey to taste

1. Cut peel from orange on a board. Save juice.
2. Chop the flesh of the orange. Put a little into a dish.
3. Layer yogurt, rhubarb, juice, orange.
4. Finish with rhubarb. Scatter hazelnuts. Drizzle with honey to taste.

YOU CAN

* skip the rhubarb – use a large orange and add granola, raisins, nuts, seeds

Berry Vitamin Boost
Just fling stuff in for a zingy start...

Natural yogurt
Runny honey
Fresh/defrosted berries

1. Mix yogurt, honey.
2. Scatter berries.

Warm Berry
A luxurious immune-boost...

Natural yogurt
Runny honey
Blueberry compote (pg 27)

1. Mix the yogurt and honey.
2. Prepare blueberry compote or reheat till warm.
3. Pour onto yogurt or swirl in.

YOU CAN

* team with plums or dried fruit salad (pg 37) (boost iron)

CEREALS

Customize your cereal so it tastes exactly as you like it and does precisely what you need it to – getting you through to the next meal without snacking.

8 Weetabix, crushed
250g/8oz All-Bran/bran flakes
250g/8oz oats, flaked/crushed
Seeds (e.g. pumpkin, sesame, poppy, sunflower)
Dried fruit (e.g. dates, apricots, cranberries, raisins, figs)
Nuts (e.g. cashews, hazelnuts, almonds, Brazils)
Fresh wheatgerm
A little organic brown sugar (optional)

Designer Muesli

Make it up a batch at a time for convenience.

1. Mix ingredients well. Chuck into jar or airtight container to store.
2. Eat with milk/soy milk, yogurt, fruit juice. Top with fresh fruit.

YOU CAN

* skip Weetabix. Substitute rye, barley – do health-store recce.
* drop in some chocolate chips, dried coconut
* melt chocolate in a bowl (pg 12). Mix in a handful or two of muesli. Tip onto baking paper/tray. Leave to set. Break bits off. Good in pack-ups.

Own Granola

Packed with energy … get it light and toasty.

MAKES
1 JAR

1. Preheat oven to 170°C/325°F/gas 3.
2. Melt honey and oil very gently in a small pan.
3. Tip into a bowl with oats, other cereal, flakes, wheatgerm.
4. Stir in dried fruit/nuts now or add after baking.
5. Spread evenly on a non-stick baking tray or baking paper on tray.
6. Bake 15–20 minutes. Turn a few times, checking the mix doesn't burn. Remove when toasty gold. Cool to crisp on the tray.
7. Add extras now if you haven't baked them in. Stores 1 month.

YOU CAN
* add 1 tbsp lemon juice at step 2
* add 2 pinches of cinnamon or drops of vanilla extract
* add cereal flakes – wheat, barley, rye, nuts, bran sticks, other dried fruit

Basic mix
2 tbsps honey
2 tbsps sunflower/vegetable oil
450g/1lb rolled/porridge oats

Extras
1 tbsp wheatgerm
Wheat flakes
Pumpkin seeds
Sesame seeds
Dates
Dried apricots
Dried cranberries
Nuts of choice
Desiccated coconut

FEEDS 1 | VEGAN OPT. | EXPRESS

50g/2oz porridge oats
330ml/½ pint water or milk/soy or
milk/water mix
Pinch salt

Tasty Porridge: Basic & Options

Keep it basic or make it luxurious – oats pack useful slow-release energy. Select extras according to season.

1. Put ingredients into pan. Bring to boil, stirring.
2. Reduce heat. Simmer, stirring, for 4 minutes or till creamy.
3. Eat as is or top with options.

OPTIONS

❋ top with sugar, honey, syrup, milk/soy, cream, yogurt

❋ **Apple:** stir in grated apple, sugar, pinch of cinnamon

❋ **Seeds:** mashed banana, pumpkin seeds, sesame seeds, sunflower seeds, nuts, dates, yogurt, honey

❋ **Tutti-frutti:** mashed banana, grated apple, sugar or honey, granola

❋ **Jamaican banana:** mashed banana, honey, cinnamon

❋ **Citrus banana:** mashed banana, lemon juice, maple syrup

❋ **Choc banana:** mashed banana, chocolate chips, syrup or honey

❋ **Stoned fruit:** roast or poached plums/peach/nectarine (pg 37), yogurt, honey

❋ **Mango:** diced mango, granola or dried coconut, maple syrup/yogurt/coconut cream

❋ **Berry:** mashed or sliced banana, any berry, dollop of yogurt, granola

Instant Bircher Muesli

Invented by a doctor, so it's got to be good for you. Keeps for a week in the fridge. Vary the toppings.

1. Chuck everything except the apple into a bowl. Stir well. Leave overnight.

2. Spoon into a breakfast bowl with extra milk or yogurt and grated apple. Stir well. Add toppings.

3. Keep remaining base in an airtight container, refrigerated.

175g/6oz oats
Handful raisins, sultanas
50g/2oz hazelnuts, chopped
200ml/7fl oz apple or orange juice
200ml/7fl oz milk/soy milk
Big squeeze lemon juice
Grated apple to serve

YOU CAN
* top base with fresh fruit, honey, yogurt
* make Fast Nut-free Oats. Mix 50g/2oz oats, 80ml/3fl oz apple juice/water, 1 grated apple, unpeeled. Leave at least 5 minutes. Add yogurt, honey, lemon in winter. In summer mash any berries in.

PER PERSON **VEGAN OPT.**

4 Irish potato cakes (see pg 28)
Oil for frying
2 good veggie sausages, chilled, not frozen
1 large open/portobello mushroom
1 large tomato, halved
1 slice bread
Heinz baked beans
2 eggs

All-Day Full English

The king of all breakfasts. Good for a Sunday morning treat – or any time. Use freshest eggs – free-range.

1. Make potato cakes (pg 28). Keep them warm.

2. Heat oil in a large pan over medium heat. Add sausages.

3. Lightly brush the mushroom with oil. Season. Add to the pan.

4. Brush the tomato halves with oil. Season. Add to the pan.

5. Turn the sausages to prevent drying out. Remove food as cooked and keep warm. Toast bread. Heat the baked beans.

6. Add more oil to the pan and increase heat. Crack the first egg. Let it slip gently out of the shell into hot fat. Repeat with second egg.

7. Flick oil over yolks with a spatula till set as you like or flip over. Remove.

8. Arrange neatly on a plate or pile high. Eat with brown sauce, ketchup.

YOU CAN

✱ fry the bread in hot oil till crisp at step 2

✱ poach the eggs (pg 31), scramble (pg 29) or make tofu scramble (pg 29)

✱ fry cold left-over potatoes at step 1 instead of potato cakes

✱ serve with rosti (pg 31) or sesame mushrooms

✱ brush tomato with oil smushed up with a bit of basil

✱ fry the eggs in a lightly oiled chef's ring

✱ make Fry-up Omelette. Get everything cooked, except eggs. Beat 2–3 eggs in a pan as you would for omelette (pg 62). Leave to set gently. Season lightly. Slide onto a plate or carve up.

American Breakfast

Another of the world's great big breakfasts.

FEEDS 4

VEGAN OPT.

1. **Chilli**: heat oil in a large pan. Fry onions, garlic very gently till soft. Add peppers. Cook for 10 minutes or till softening. Add remaining ingredients. Boil. Simmer on low for 20 minutes. Season.

2. Meantime, boil chopped potatoes in lightly salted water for 10 minutes. Drain. Fry slowly in hot oil, turning, until browned, crispy.

3. Prep guacamole and salsa. Scramble eggs or tofu (pg 29).

4. Warm tortillas a few seconds per side in a dry pan/griddle/oven.

5. Assemble: spoon a line of chilli into tortillas. Roll or wrap. Serve with crispy spuds, eggs/tofu, guacamole, salsa, chunk of lime, sour cream.

1 x Veggie Chilli (pg 120)
3 medium potatoes, peeled, and chopped
Oil for frying
Guacamole (pg 52)
Salsa (pg 52)
Scrambled egg x 4 or tofu (pg 29)
4 tortillas
1 lime, quartered
Sour cream

YOU CAN

* make Breakfast Burritos. Spoon hot chilli, scrambled egg, grated Cheddar, hot pepper sauce into warmed tortillas. Roll into cones.

* wrap filled, rolled tortillas in foil (with or without egg). Heat a griddle pan. Griddle a few minutes per side till marked/hot through. Peel foil back to eat.

* use chilli re-fried beans

* make Huveos Rancheros. Spread hot chilli in a heatproof dish. Crack 4 eggs into dents in surface. Bake at 200°C/400°F/ gas 6 till eggs are set. Eat with Cheddar, tortillas etc.

TOAST... with stuff on top

Homestyle Baked Beans on Toast

Run out of Heinz? Try these out for size.

- **1 tbsp olive/sunflower oil**
- **1 small onion, finely chopped**
- **1 clove garlic, crushed**
- **1 x 200g/7oz can tomatoes**
- **150ml/5fl oz hot water mixed with pinch Marigold vegetable stock or own stock (pg 184)**
- **2 tsps tomato purée**
- **1–2 tsps mustard**
- **2 shakes soy sauce**
- **Shake Henderson's Relish/ Tabasco**
- **1 tbsp brown sugar**
- **1 x 400g/14oz can cannellini/ haricot beans**
- **2 slices good bread**

1. Fry the onion very gently in hot oil for 5 minutes. Add the garlic. Cook till softened, not coloured.

2. Add tomatoes, stock, soy sauce, tomato purée. Simmer gently for 10–15 minutes.

3. Add mustard, Henderson's sauce, sugar, beans. Simmer for 5 minutes.

4. Taste and adjust seasoning. Toast bread. Pile the beans on.

Cherry Tomato Bruschetta

Simple but beautiful – best in summer when tomatoes are in season.

- **2 slices baguette/ciabatta**
- **Olive oil**
- **Garlic clove, cut**
- **Handful cherry tomatoes**
- **Salt and pepper**
- **Fresh basil**

1. Preheat a griddle pan till it's scorching hot.

2. Rub sliced bread with olive oil and cut side of garlic clove.

3. Sit bread on griddle till crisp, cooked, marked.

4. Turn. Meantime, chop tomatoes. Toss in a bit of oil, seasoning, torn basil. Top the hot bread.

YOU CAN

* add chopped garlic
* add chopped mozzarella
* use chopped vine tomatoes
* grill if no griddle
* drizzle any toast with olive oil. Rub with garlic, then a halved tomato.

Mushrooms on Toast

Cheap, easy and pretty damned tasty – sesame seeds make all the difference.

- **1 slice brown/white bread**
- **Butter/oil**
- **Handful white button/chestnut mushrooms**
- **Shake soy sauce/tamari**
- **Black pepper**
- **A few sesame seeds**

1. Slice mushrooms. Fry in butter/oil till tender.

2. Pile onto buttered toast. Season with soy, pepper, seeds.

YOU CAN

* make it exotic. Chop 150g/5oz exotic mushrooms. Fry slowly in butter/oil with crushed garlic. Turn carefully. Add optional squeeze of lemon, splash of mushroom ketchup, thyme, seasoning. Tip onto toast with juices.

French Toast & Blueberries

Rich, decadent – a prime dish for breakfast in bed treatment. Enjoy with a cup of Earl Grey or a proper coffee.

1. Crack eggs into a shallow bowl. Beat in the sour cream, sugar, cinnamon.

2. Dip the first slice of bread into the mix to soak. Turn. Repeat with the second slice.

3. Melt the butter in a frying pan. When bubbling, put the eggy bread in and fry each side till crisp and golden.

4. Meantime, heat the blueberries in a small pan with sugar and lemon juice. Heat till they're just soft.

5. Serve bread with maple syrup, icing sugar, blueberries.

2 eggs
2 tbsps sour cream
½–1 tbsp caster sugar
Good pinch cinnamon
2 slices white bread, crusts removed
A little butter
Maple syrup
Icing sugar

Blueberry compôte
50g/2oz blueberries
1 tbsp caster sugar
Squeeze lemon juice

YOU CAN

✱ add vanilla extract and cinnamon to egg mix

✱ use stale bread or brioche

✱ use milk instead of sour cream

✱ make Banana French Toast. Soak in egg mix. Fry till golden on each side. Bake 10 minutes at 180°C/350°F/gas 4.

✱ fry sandwiches made with sweetened cream cheese, chopped walnuts

✱ soak crustless cheese sandwiches in egg, milk, mustard, and bake in a greased shallow dish at 180°C/350°F/gas 4 for 10 minutes or until cooked through/crispy

✱ vegans – soak bread in soy milk, sugar and vanilla extract, and fry in soy margarine till golden

✱ serve the compôte with ice-cream, yogurt

250g/9oz potatoes (peeled weight)
25g/1oz butter
50g/2oz plain flour
A little salt
A few chives or spring-onion tops, snipped (optional)
Extra flour for dry-frying

Irish Potato Cakes

A great breakfast component – these little cakes soak up the juices.

1. Boil potatoes till tender. Drain. Put into a sieve/colander over the warm pan. Cover. Leave for 5 minutes. Mash till smooth.
2. Melt butter. Tip into a bowl with mash, flour, salt, chives/onion tops. Mix gently with a fork. Pull lightly into a warm dough.
3. Place on a lightly floured surface. Roll out gently till 1cm/½in thick. Cut into small circles with a cutter, or into triangles.
4. Sprinkle extra flour into a hot frying pan. When slightly browned, cook cakes a few minutes each side till brown and cooked through.

YOU CAN
* cut into 4 larger cakes. Cook. Eat hot, with butter, jam, lemon curd (pg 187).
* make with non-dairy spread for vegan option
* make Skint Apple Turnovers. Roll potato dough into 4 x 15cm/6in circles. Cover half of each circle with thinly sliced apple, cinnamon, sugar. Fold the other half over. Press edges to seal. Cook on pan as above on v low heat 15 minutes per side or until apple is cooked.

2 medium potatoes, peeled
1 medium onion
1 egg
Salt and pepper
2 tbsps oil

Hash Browns

Squeeze out as much moisture as you can for lovely crisp hash browns. Enjoy with UK and US breakfasts.

1. Grate potatoes and onion onto a clean tea towel.
2. Twist hard to squeeze moisture out. Tip into bowl.
3. Mix in egg, seasoning. Heat oil in pan.
4. Fill cooking rings 1cm/½in deep with the hash, or roughly shape it in a pan. Fry 5–10 minutes per side till golden.

Scrambled Eggs

Eggs are the ultimate fast food and an easy source of protein. Scramble carefully and they can taste extraordinary. My sister Polly lived on these at Uni.

2 large eggs
Salt and black pepper
Knob of butter

1. Crack eggs into a bowl. Beat well with a fork. Season.
2. Tip butter and eggs into a cold pan. Sit over a very low heat.
3. For creamy eggs: stir constantly with a wooden spoon till done as you like. Get onto plate at once as they keep cooking. For more textured eggs: stir, leave a few seconds to shape, stir again, leave again, repeating for a shapely scramble. Eat on toast, muffin, bagel.

YOU CAN
* make Cheese Eggs. Add grated Cheddar just as eggs set.
* make Blow-Out Scramble. At step 3 stir in 1 tsp Dijon mustard, 1–2 tbsps grated Gruyère/Cheddar, dash cream/mayo, fine herbs/chopped spring-onion tops.
* make Chilli Eggs. Fry a little very finely chopped onion, garlic, chilli in butter. Add eggs, optional coriander. Season. Scramble. Serve with optional sour cream.
* top with cooked asparagus/tenderstem broccoli, roasted vine tomatoes (pg 184)

Scrambled Tofu

Tofu's a top source of calcium and protein. Here's how my vegan sister KR cooks it for breakfast. You can also use firm tofu.

1 pack tofu
2–3 spring onions, chopped
1 clove garlic, chopped
½ small red pepper, diced
Oil for frying
3 pinches turmeric
1–2 tbsps soy sauce/tamari
Pinch cayenne
Fresh coriander (optional)

1. Drain and crumble the tofu.
2. Gently fry the spring onion, garlic, red pepper in 2 tbsps hot oil, stirring till soft.
3. Add the tofu, turmeric, soy sauce or tamari, cayenne. Turn till hot. Add fresh coriander if available.

YOU CAN
* slap into Breakfast Burritos (pg 25)

2 eggs
1 tsp chopped parsley
1 tsp torn basil
1 tsp water
2 pinches salt and a little pepper
A little olive oil

Omelette aux Fines Herbes

A simple speedy French classic – why not grow the herbs on your windowsill so you've always got some in?

1. Put the eggs, herbs, water and seasoning into a bowl and beat with a whisk or fork until all the ingredients are combined.

2. Put a little oil into a non-stick 6in frying pan over a high heat.

3. When it's almost smoking, put the egg mixture in.

4. Immediately get a spatula and pull the setting egg mixture back on one side and tilt the runny mixture into its place. Continue to do this until it's all set.

5. Place your hand palm upwards under the frying-pan handle and tilt it up, easing the omelette out onto a plate while it's still soft.

YOU CAN

* add a little grated cheese or mustard to the egg mix
* place the omelette in a baguette with a squeeze of tomato ketchup for a quick sandwich
* fry onion and garlic till golden. Add eggs.
* add a little feta cheese, black olives, diced tomato
* add cubes of hot fried bread and chopped herbs
* add lightly fried banana, squeeze of lemon
* omit herbs – drizzle balsamic vinegar or honey

Rosti with Poached Egg

This one's inspired by a Swiss classic served at the famous Betty's Tea Rooms in Yorkshire, and is something I've been eating and loving for years. Topping rosti with a poached egg makes for a perfect relaxed breakfast.

FEEDS 2   VEGAN OPT.

2 large potatoes in their skins
Salt and pepper
Spring onion, chopped (optional)
Oil or oil and butter for frying
2 eggs
Pinch salt

1. Boil potatoes in water for 5–10 minutes until just tender.
2. Drain. Leave to cool completely or till you can handle them.
3. Strip off the peel. Grate roughly into a bowl. Season. Add optional onion.
4. Heat oil or oil and butter. Shape handfuls of mix into thin cakes (do this in the pan if very crumbly). Fry each side for 5 minutes or until golden.
5. Meantime, boil a saucepan or frying pan of water. Add salt. Crack first egg into a cup.
6. Stir water fast, creating a whirlpool. Tip egg into the centre to shape it.
7. Simmer 3–4 minutes or till the white is set, the yolk still soft inside. Remove with a slotted spoon, allowing the water to drain. Trim whites if you need. Place on a rosti. Season. Repeat with second egg.

YOU CAN
* boil potatoes ahead in skins, grate from cold for express rosti
* add lightly fried onion, garlic, fresh herbs to rosti mix
* make one big rosti to fill the pan. Cook 10 minutes each side, using plate to help turn it over.
* top rosti with crumbled goat's cheese and dressed salad leaves
* vegans – top with mushrooms (pg 26) and panfried tofu (pg 29)
* griddle a mushroom – add to the pile
* grate Cheddar or Gruyère cheese over the egg
* sit egg on salad with hot crispy potatoes
* sit egg on a bowl of cheese and onion mash (pg 162–3)

Handful spinach leaves
1–2 eggs
Pinch nutmeg (optional)

Cheese sauce
25g/1oz butter
25g/1oz flour
300ml/½ pint milk
Handful strong Cheddar, grated
Salt and pepper
A little mustard (optional)
Squeeze lemon juice (optional)

Eggs Florentine

Packed full of iron and great taste. Grill it for speed or you can bake it – a lovely late breakfast.

1. Wash spinach. Tip into pan with a few drops of water. Cook for a few minutes until the leaves wilt and soften. Drain. Set aside.

2. Melt butter in the pan. Stir in the flour and cook for 1–2 minutes.

3. Beat or whisk in the milk very gradually for a smooth sauce. Cook on a low heat, stirring, till it boils and thickens. Simmer for 5 minutes.

4. Add the cheese, seasoning, optional mustard and lemon juice. Taste and adjust.

5. Poach eggs (pg 31). Season the spinach, adding optional nutmeg.

6. Put spinach into a shallow ovenproof dish, top with egg. Season.

7. Cover with sauce. Finish under a preheated grill for a few minutes until hot and bubbling, removing before the egg yolk sets.

YOU CAN
* bake in a hot oven till bubbling
* cover eggs with crème fraîche mixed with grated cheese and mustard. Grill.
* team with soda bread (pg 97)
* make more sauce – use half for mac cheese (pg 110) or lasagne topping (pg 113)
* make Swiss Baked Eggs. Grease ramekins or cups. Spoon in a bit of cream. Crack an egg in. Season. Add cream to cover. Sit cups in roasting tray, half-filled with boiling water. Bake 8–10 minutes till whites set, yolks still runny. Sprinkle with grated cheese. Grill on baking tray till bubbling. Eat with toast fingers.

Mushroom Kedgeree

A veggie version of a Scots/
Indian classic – it's hearty yet
delicate.

1. Put a pan of lightly salted
water on high heat.
2. Add the rice to the water
once it boils. Cover the pan.
Simmer on the lowest heat for
15 minutes or till soft. Test a
grain after 10 minutes. Drain
when cooked. Cover with a tea
towel.
3. Meantime, put the eggs
into a small pan of salted cold
water. Bring to the boil and
cook for 8 minutes. Remove.
Plunge into a bowl of cold water. Tap the eggs to crack. Gently
peel the shell away.
4. Melt the butter gently in a frying pan. Add the garlic and
mushrooms. Turn until just tender. Add the cooked rice and peas
with a pinch of cayenne. Turn gently for a few minutes till heated
through. Pile onto warmed plates.
5. Top with half the egg, parsley, a few shakes of soy, and a dollop
of sour cream or mayo. Serve with chunk of lemon if you like.

YOU CAN
* add a pinch of curry powder
* add lightly fried onion
* stir in a few cooked lentils/quinoa
* use brown rice but cook it for longer
* add a little cream to the rice mix
* top with cashews/stir-fried tofu

FEEDS 4   VEGAN OPT.

Pinch salt
200g/7oz basmati rice, rinsed in cold
  water
2–3 eggs
Bit of butter
1 clove garlic, crushed
2–3 portobello/large open
  mushrooms, sliced thickly
A few shiitake/white/chestnut
  mushrooms, sliced
Handful cooked peas
Pinch cayenne pepper
A little fresh parsley, finely chopped
Shake soy sauce
Dollop sour cream or mayo or soy
  cream
Chunk lemon (optional)

FEEDS 4

EXPRESS

VEGAN OPT.

110g/4oz plain flour
Pinch salt
1 large egg
300ml/½ pint milk
Splash water
1 tbsp sunflower oil/melted butter
Butter for frying

Topping options
Caster sugar and lemon juice
Maple syrup and orange juice
Chocolate spread
Melted jam
Nutella
Cheddar/Gruyère cheese, grated

Pancakes

If the first pancake sticks, don't worry. Chuck it away and start over. A perfect breakfast for when you've got mates round – everyone, customize the toppings.

1. Sift the flour and salt into a bowl. Make a hollow in it.

2. Crack the egg into the hollow. Add a good glug of milk.

3. Start beating hard using a balloon whisk or wooden spoon. Add the rest of the milk slowly, beating continuously to get a smooth batter. Stir in the water and oil/melted butter.

4. Heat a frying pan till very hot. Add a little butter.

5. Pour or spoon in 2–3 tbsps batter. Swirl the pan again to make a big thin crêpe. Cook for 1 min or till it sets. Toss, or turn with a spatula. Cook other side.

YOU CAN

＊ vegans – mix flour, salt, 2 tsps baking powder, 4 tbsps veg oil, soy milk for batter or use soy and egg substitute with standard recipe

＊ sub a bit of the flour with cocoa for choc ones

＊ freeze pancakes

＊ make mix night before

US-Style Pancakes

Lighter than drop scones,
fatter than normal
pancakes. Stack 'em high
and enjoy yourselves.

1. Sift the flour, sugar, salt,
baking powder into a large
bowl.

2. Beat egg yolks, milk, butter
in another. Then beat very
slowly into the dry
ingredients, using a balloon
whisk or wooden spoon, for
a smooth batter.

3. Whisk the egg whites till
stiff, using a grease-free whisk.
Then lightly fold into the
batter with a large metal spoon.

4. Brush a large heated frying pan with melted butter.

5. Drop individual tablespoons of mix into the pan, leaving room
for expansion. Cook till the base browns and bubbles
appear on the surface (1–2 minutes). Turn. Cook till golden.

YOU CAN
* put a handful of blueberries into the mix
* grate in a little apple for a Polish version
* add a pinch of cinnamon or vanilla extract
* eat with melted butter and honey/jam
* eat with chopped banana and melted golden syrup
* eat with apple slices fried in a little butter, lemon juice, sugar

FEEDS 4   EXPRESS

110g/4oz plain flour
10g/½oz caster sugar
Pinch salt
2 tsps baking powder
2 large eggs, separated (pg 11)
150ml/½ pint milk
50g/2oz melted butter
Extra melted butter

Stacking
Fresh berries
Maple/golden syrup
Lemon juice

Grilled Grapefruit

You don't have to be a grapefruit fan to like this. It loses most of its acidity and is just beautiful to eat.

1. Preheat the grill.
2. Sit grapefruit on base. Cut across the centre, horizontally.
3. Cut around the segments with a sharp knife to loosen.
4. Sprinkle with brown sugar (white also works).
5. Sit fruit under the heat till it bubbles (2 minutes).

FEEDS 1   VEGAN   EXPRESS

1 red/pink/yellow grapefruit
Sprinkling of brown sugar

YOU CAN
* sprinkle a bit of cinnamon and top with a dot of butter
* grill halved stoned plums or peaches – sit on a baking tray

Freestyle Fruit Salad

See what's in the fruit bowl and in season. Get your fruit cheaper from local markets. A vitamin C fest.

FEEDS 1   VEGAN   EXPRESS

Choice of seasonal fruit
Green and red grapes, kiwi fruit, pineapple, melon, satsuma, mango, pear, apple, raspberries, strawberries, orange, banana, blackberries

Peel. Chop. Slice. Tip into a bowl with runaway juices.

YOU CAN
* add apple/orange juice or weak elderflower cordial for instant syrup
* make a syrup. Boil up 300ml/10fl oz water, 110g/4oz sugar for 5 minutes. Cool it.
* slice up a melon or watermelon if no time for chopping. It's light to eat, heavy on energy.
* squeeze an orange for freshest home-style OJ

Dried Fruit Salad

Packed with iron and other nutrients – keep a store in the fridge during winter when fresh isn't best.

1. Chop apricots, prunes or leave whole. Add any optional extras. Cover with boiling water and soak overnight.

2. Drain, saving water. Put fruit into a large pan with honey and soaking water to cover. Boil then reduce heat.

3. Simmer for 30 minutes or till soft. Cool. Eat warm/chilled. Eat with yogurt, sprinkled nuts (walnuts, hazelnuts, almonds, pistachios).

YOU CAN

✱ add dried bananas, apples, pears, figs, plums at step 1

✱ layer up with yogurt, honey, chopped orange

✱ cook for longer in very little liquid – mash up to eat with bread and cheese as chutney

✱ store for 4 weeks in a sealed jar/container

MAKES 1 JAR   VEGAN

175g/6oz dried apricots
175g/6oz prunes

Optional extras
Raisins/sultanas
Dried cranberries
Dates
Honey
Orange juice/squeeze of lemon

Poached Plums

Love the liquor. This doubles up as a refreshing breakfast and a great dessert.

1. Heat water and sugar in a pan large enough to take plums.

2. When sugar dissolves, add plums and extras.

3. Reduce heat. Simmer very gently for 10–15 minutes till skins split and plums tenderize. Eat hot, warm, cold.

YOU CAN

✱ poach apricots, nectarines, or mix the fruit

✱ top with almonds, pistachios, yogurt

✱ eat with custard (pg 187) or vanilla ice-cream after dinner

FEEDS 2-3   VEGAN   EXPRESS

240ml/8fl oz water
110g/4oz caster sugar
450g/1lb plums
1 tsp rosewater (optional)
1 small sprig rosemary (optional)
1 vanilla pod/5 drops vanilla extract

LUNCHES
& LIGHT BITES

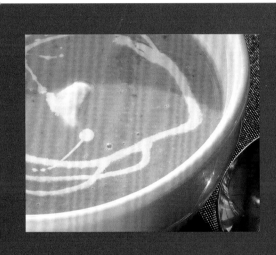

SOUPS

Soup through the seasons. Make with your own stock or Marigold and feel free to freestyle with spare veg, beans or pasta. Eat in, with bread, or take out.

Leek & Potato

A family favourite and well cheap. Use the basic method to knock out loads of variations. Cut veg small.

Feeds 2–3

- 50g/2oz butter
- 110g/4oz onion, chopped very finely
- 450g/1lb floury potatoes (e.g. 4 medium-size Maris Piper, King Edwards), peeled
- 1–2 leeks, v thinly sliced
- 850ml/1½ pints water mixed with ½ tsp Marigold bouillon/ own veg stock (pg 184)
- A few sprigs fresh parsley
- 3 tbsps milk
- Salt and pepper
- Sundried tomato, finely diced (optional)

1. Dice potatoes into v small chunks.

2. Melt butter in pan. Add onions, pinch salt.
3. Cook, stirring, for 1 minute. Stir in potatoes, leeks. Cover with greaseproof paper and lid. Cook gently for 10 minutes without colouring.
4. Remove paper. Add Marigold mix/ stock. Boil. Reduce heat. Simmer gently for 10 minutes. Remove from heat.
5. Add parsley. Blitz till smooth with a handblender (or mash or sieve).
6. Stir in milk, seasoning. Reheat. Serve as is or with diced sundried tomato. Eat with Cheese Fat Rascal (pg 95).

YOU CAN

✳ make it Potato and Onion soup – omit leeks

✳ sub in any sliced/diced veg for leeks, e.g. 3 handfuls shredded cabbage/spinach

✳ add in chopped watercress/lemon juice/mustard/grated cheese

✳ add in 250g/10oz mushrooms, garlic, rosemary

✳ sprinkle spring onions, crumbled blue cheese, diced fried bread

Beetroot Soup

Unmatchable for colour and pretty damned tasty. Note: also great for you – loads of folate.

Feeds 2–3

- 1 onion, finely chopped
- 1 clove garlic, crushed
- A bit of butter or olive oil
- 2 tsps sugar
- 1 potato, peeled, chopped small
- 4 pre-cooked plain beetroot in vacuum pack
- A little fresh ginger, grated
- Juice of ½ orange (or slurp from carton)
- Salt and black pepper
- 1–1½ pints water
- A little sugar
- Lemon juice/wine vinegar to taste

To finish

- Dab of yogurt, cream or sour cream

1. Gently fry the onion and garlic in melted butter or oil in a pan.
2. When soft, not coloured, add the potato. Continue to cook gently till softening.

Mulligatawny

Curry soup – as simple as…

Feeds 4–6

1 large onion, finely chopped
Pinch salt
1 tbsp butter/groundnut oil
2–3 cloves garlic, crushed
2.5cm/1in ginger, grated
2 tsps korma/other good curry paste
50g/2oz red lentils, rinsed
1 x 400g/14oz can chopped tomatoes
450g/1lb courgettes, chopped
1 large sweet potato, peeled, chopped
1–2 litres/2 pints veg stock/ water or 1 tsp Marigold bouillon in water
1–2 tsps mango chutney
Fresh coriander
Squeeze lemon juice

1. Cook onion, salt in butter/oil over gentle heat for 3 minutes.
2. Add garlic, ginger, curry paste. Stir well. Cook for 6 minutes.
3. Add lentils. Stir in tomatoes, courgettes, potato. Reduce heat. Cover. Simmer v gently for 15 minutes.
4. Add stock, chutney, a bit of coriander. Cover. Cook 10–15 minutes. Adjust taste with lemon juice or chutney.
5. Blend in the pan with handblender. Add water if it's too thick.

YOU CAN
✱ top with poppadoms, homemade yogurt (pg 18) and coriander
✱ make or heat up some naan bread (pg 130)

---

3. Add the chopped beetroot, ginger, orange, a little salt, and add water to cover. Boil. Reduce. Simmer 15 minutes.
4. Add sugar, seasoning and blend or blitz with a handblender till smooth.
5. Taste, adding a little juice or wine vinegar. Blitz and reheat.

Pea & Chilli

A brilliant little soup for all times of the year. Chilli makes it refreshing yet warming. Use frozen peas for the freshest flavour.

Feeds 2–3

3 tbsps butter
110g/4oz onion, finely chopped
2 cloves garlic, finely chopped
1 mild green chilli, de-seeded, finely chopped
450g/1lb frozen peas
1½ pints light vegetable stock, heated
2½ tbsps chopped fresh coriander
Seasoning including sugar

1. Melt butter until it foams. Sweat onion, garlic and chilli over gentle heat and season.
2. Once onion is soft add the peas. Cover with the hot stock. Boil. Simmer for 6 minutes, uncovered.
3. When peas are cooked, add coriander and liquidize until completely smooth. Season to taste and serve.

YOU CAN
✱ add a swirl of softly whipped cream and a few pea shoots on top, for a bistro look
✱ top with a bit of toast or croûton with a poached egg on top
✱ add 1 tbsp fresh/a bit of dried mint instead of chilli

Thai-Style Roasted Squash

A lovely spicy warming bowlful. Play with flavourings so it's not too sweet…

Feeds 6

- **700g/1½lb butternut squash, peeled, cut into large bits**
- **Olive oil**
- **25g/1oz butter**
- **1 medium onion, finely chopped**
- **2 fat cloves garlic, crushed**
- **10cm/4in piece fresh ginger, grated**
- **Juice of 2 limes**
- **850ml/1½ pints veg stock**
- **50g/2oz piece creamed coconut dissolved in 300ml/ ½ pint boiling water**
- **Fresh coriander**
- **Salt and pepper**
- **Tabasco sauce (optional)**
- **Balsamic vinegar (optional)**

1. Preheat oven to 200°C/400°F/gas 6. Drizzle oil over squash on a baking tray.

2. Roast 30 minutes or till soft. Meantime, melt butter in a large pan.

3. Fry onion and garlic v gently for 5 minutes or till soft, not coloured.

4. Add ginger for another minute.

5. Add cooked squash, lime, stock, coconut, coriander, salt, pepper.

6. Stir as you bring to the boil. Reduce heat. Cover. Simmer gently for 15 minutes, adding extra water if needed.

7. Blend or blitz with a handblender. Taste, adjust with lime, Tabasco, balsamic to balance out the sweetness.

YOU CAN

✱ crumble 1–2 dried chillies or flakes at step 1

✱ add 1 tbsp cooked chickpeas after blitzing

✱ crumble on a bit of goat's cheese

Tomato & Lentil

My mum invented this yummy soup when my brother was young to get some vegetables down him. Adding the lentils packs in texture and protein.

Feeds 4–6

- **1–2 tbsps olive oil**
- **1 large onion, finely chopped**
- **3–4 cloves garlic, crushed**
- **½ large chilli, de-seeded, finely chopped**
- **1 potato, peeled, chopped v small**
- **1 carrot, peeled, chopped v small**
- **200g/7oz red lentils, rinsed**
- **2 x 400g/14oz cans chopped tomatoes**
- **1½ litres/2½ pints vegetable stock/water or 1 tsp Marigold bouillon in water**
- **2–3 tbsps tomato purée**
- **Pinch of sugar**
- **1–2 tbsps fresh parsley/ coriander, chopped**
- **Squeeze lemon juice**
- **Salt and black pepper**
- **Splash mushroom ketchup (optional)**
- **A few drops Tabasco (optional)**

1. Heat oil in a large pan. Add the onion, garlic and a pinch of salt. Fry very gently until soft, not coloured.

2. After 1 minute add the potato, carrot. Cover. Sweat very gently for 10 minutes. Stir in the rinsed lentils, tomatoes, stock, purée, sugar, seasoning. Simmer for 15–20 minutes or till the veg are very soft.

3. Taste, add optional extras and adjust seasoning. Serve chunky or blend till smooth. Add water or purée till right. Great with bread, cheese.

Minestrone

Gorgeous Italian soup with a tomato base. Chuck in all your left-over pasta.

Feeds 2–3

1–2 tbsps oil
1 onion, sliced into rings
3 cloves garlic
1 large potato, peeled, diced
2 small sticks celery, sliced
1 carrot, peeled, sliced
1 leek, sliced
Handful green beans, cut into
**   thirds**
Salt and black pepper
1.5 litres/2½ pints vegetable
**   stock/weak Marigold bouillon**
1 x 400g/14oz can chopped
**   tomatoes**
2–3 tbsps tomato purée
Pinch dried thyme/oregano
1 tsp sugar
2 handfuls macaroni
Bit of spaghetti
½ x 400g/14oz can butterbeans
1 courgette, diced
A little shredded cabbage
**   (optional)**
A few basil leaves/bit of
**   chopped parsley**
Garlic bread (pg 187)

1. Heat oil in a large pan. Add onion and garlic. Cook gently for 5 minutes, stirring, till soft.
2. Add potato, celery, carrot, leek,

beans, salt and pepper. Simmer, stirring, till soft and translucent.
3. Add stock/bouillon, tomatoes, purée, dried herbs, sugar. Boil. Reduce heat.
4. Simmer gently 30–40 minutes.
5. Increase heat. Add macaroni. Boil 5–10 minutes.
6. Add the spaghetti and butterbeans. Boil. Add courgette after 5 minutes. Simmer 5 minutes.
7. Add shredded cabbage to wilt with basil/parsley. Taste. Adjust seasoning.
8. Serve with grated Parmesan or Cheddar and garlic bread.

YOU CAN

✳ use other beans and pasta shapes
✳ drizzle in a bit of balsamic/pesto
✳ add a bit of crème fraîche to left-overs, stir into pasta

Carrot & Coriander

So good for you, it's almost indecent!

Feeds 4

50g/2oz butter
1 onion, finely chopped
700g/1½lb carrots, peeled
225g/8oz potatoes, peeled
Bunch fresh coriander, chopped
850ml/1½ pints vegetable stock
125ml/4fl oz coconut milk
Juice of 1 orange
Salt and black pepper
Good squeeze of lime/lemon
**   juice**
2 limes/lemons, cut into
**   wedges (optional)**

1. Melt butter in a pan. Cook onion gently till soft, not coloured.
2. Chop carrots and potatoes into small bits. Add to the pan.

3. Stir, cover with greaseproof and lid and leave to sweat for 10 minutes.
4. Add coriander, stock, coconut milk, orange juice, lemon/lime juice, salt and pepper. Bring to the boil. Reduce heat to low and simmer 30–40 minutes or till the carrots are soft.
5. Blend or blitz with a handblender. Reheat gently, taste, adjust seasoning. Serve with optional lime to squeeze at table. Eat with bread for balance.

Veggie Ramen

Eat your heart out, Pot Noodle. Vary the veg to suit taste and budget.

Feeds 1

- ½ 250g/9oz pack firm tofu, prepped and cubed (pg 12)
- 1 nest noodles (egg, soba, whatever)
- Vegetable and/or sesame oil for frying

Marinade

- 2 tbsps hoisin sauce
- 1 tbsp veggie oyster sauce
- 2 tsps rice wine

Vegetables

- Mushrooms, thinly sliced
- Chinese leaf/iceberg lettuce, chopped
- Pak choi, chopped
- A few beansprouts
- 3 spring onions, thinly sliced
- 1 chilli, de-seeded, thinly sliced

Stock

- 1 litre/1¾ pints hot water with 2 tsps Marigold bouillon or 1 litre/1¾ pints own vegetable stock or water with miso
- Salt and pepper

Chilli Dressing sauce

- 1 tsp caster sugar
- 2½ tbsps soy sauce
- 1½ tbsps rice/malt vinegar
- 1 tbsp chilli sauce

1. Prep tofu (pg 12). Stir to coat in mixed marinade ingredients. Leave for 30 minutes.
2. Prepare vegetables and stock. Cook noodles for 3–4 minutes in boiling water. Drain well.
3. Heat oil in a hot pan. Pan-fry tofu, turning to cook each side till hot (4 minutes).
4. After 3 minutes, add the mushrooms and remaining marinade.
5. Remove tofu and mushrooms. Stir noodles into remaining sauce to coat. Remove.
6. De-glaze pan by adding a ladle of stock, stirring, to capture sauce and flavours.
7. Add remaining stock. Bring to boil. Taste, season and adjust.
8. Drop noodles into a bowl. Add green veg, beansprouts, chilli, mushrooms. Pour soup in.
9. Top with tofu and spring onions. Drizzle with Chilli Dressing sauce or leave as is.
10. Eat with a Chinese spoon and chopsticks. Serve with green tea.

YOU CAN

✳ use Chinese dried black fungus – soak in hot water 30 minutes
✳ add seaweed or fresh coriander
✳ simmer stock with sliced ginger and garlic for 30 minutes to flavour
✳ tip hot miso soup over cooked noodles in bowl. Add sliced veg (spinach, pak choi, Chinese leaf, cos/iceberg lettuce, spring or red onion).

Fast Tomato

Everyone loves tomato soup. Make up this taste of home from your basic store cupboard.

Feeds 3

- 1 medium onion, finely chopped
- 1 clove garlic, crushed

1 tbsp oil
1 x 400g/14oz can tomatoes
600ml/1 pint vegetable stock
   (own or mix ½ tsp Marigold
   bouillon in boiling water)
1 tbsp tomato purée
35g/1½oz crustless bread
Fresh basil leaves or pinch
   dried oregano
Salt and black pepper

Optional Toppings
   Finely diced red pepper
   Cucumber
   Hard-boiled egg
   Fried bread
   Torn basil

1. Cook onion, garlic gently with oil in pan for 5 minutes till soft, not coloured. Add all other ingredients. Boil 1 minute.

2. Reduce heat. Simmer gently 20 minutes. Taste. Adjust seasoning. Blitz in pan or jug with handblender or leave it rough. Reheat gently.

3. Serve topped with extras or plate them for the table.

YOU CAN

✱ add shake Tabasco

✱ stir in own or bought pesto, diced Cheddar, fried bread

✱ make Roast Tomato soup. Drizzle oil over 900g/2lb ripe tomatoes, 1 head garlic, 2 quartered red onions, dried thyme/oregano, 2 de-seeded red peppers. Bake 30–40 minutes at 220°C/425°F/gas 7. Smush garlic from skins. Blitz everything with 350ml/12fl oz hot veg stock. Add wine vinegar, Tabasco, Henderson's Relish to taste.

Gazpacho

Cool summer option – no cooking.

   900g/2lb ripe tomatoes
   1 red pepper, de-seeded,
      chopped
   1 small onion/4 spring onions,
      chopped
   ½ cucumber, peeled, diced
   4 fat cloves garlic, crushed
   1 tsp fresh thyme/basil leaves
   Salt and pepper
   Pinch of sugar
   1 tbsp red wine or sherry vinegar
   3 tbsps olive oil
   250–350ml/8–12fl oz cold water

Choice of Toppings
   Finely chopped spring onion
   Hard-boiled egg
   Red pepper
   Diced fried bread
   Diced cucumber
   Ice cubes

1. Peel tomatoes: pour boiling water over them in a bowl. Remove after 2 minutes. Peel the skins off. Quarter. Remove and discard seeds.

2. Put chopped tomatoes, red pepper, onion, cucumber, garlic, herbs, salt and pepper, sugar, vinegar and oil into a blender. Blitz till smooth.

3. Add water until you get the taste and consistency you like. Adjust seasoning.

4. Chill for 2 hours. Serve with toppings/ice cubes.

HOT ROLLS, SARNIES & PITTAS

Classic lunchtime fodder – team with soups and salads for balance. Vary breads – try making your own stuff.

5. Sit rocket on the base. Top with mushrooms. Drizzle with balsamic.

6. Leave open or top with more bread.

YOU CAN

❋ top and bake with Welsh Rarebit mix (pg 50) or sliced Brie or blue cheese

❋ stack cooked mushroom, fried egg (pg 24–25), fried or fresh tomato into a warm burger bun with green leaves

Hot Dog

Tomato ketchup
Dijon/other mustard
A little runny honey
1–2 good veggie sausages (chilled, not cook-from-frozen)
Bread roll/baguette

Choice of stackings
Mustard
Mayo
Apple chutney (pg 184)
Cucumber pickle (pg 185)
Chilli sauce
Salad leaves
Red onion, thinly sliced, raw/lightly fried
Dill pickle
Sliced tomato
Grated Cheddar

1. Mix a bit of ketchup and mustard in a bowl. Add a little honey (go easy, it burns). Taste for balance. Brush

Mushroom, Rocket & Balsamic

2 portobello mushrooms
2 cloves garlic, crushed
Salt and pepper
Olive oil/butter
2 good squeezes lemon juice
Ciabatta/good-quality bread
Rocket
Balsamic vinegar

1. Preheat oven to 230°C/450°F/gas 8.

2. Wipe mushrooms, remove stalks, prick all over with a fork.

3. Mix garlic, salt, pepper and enough oil or soft butter to spread over tops of mushrooms. Squeeze juice. Bake on a tray for 10 minutes (or grill slowly).

4. After 5 minutes, griddle, grill or toast bread.

half of it over the bangers. Chill till needed.

2. Cook under medium grill, turning till cooked (read pack instructions for timing). Brush with remaining marinade.

3. Put into warmed rolls/bread, with relishes and salad.

YOU CAN

* eat in a wrap with fried red onion and a fried egg
* cook more bangers and keep to chop on lunch salad box.
* make Bangers & Mash with onion gravy (pg 184)

Chip Butty

1–2 fresh spuds, peeled (or use cold boiled spuds/roasties)
Olive oil
Salt
Malt vinegar
2 slices any bread
Ketchup or brown sauce

1. Cut uncooked spuds into big wedges.
2. Shallow fry in oil for 10 minutes, turning, till well browned.
3. Drain on kitchen paper. Sprinkle with salt, vinegar. Pile into bread with ketchup or brown sauce.

YOU CAN

* eat as bread and butter with chips. Poach/fry an egg with it (pg 24–25).

Omelette Baguette with Green Leaves

1 baguette
2 large eggs
Salt and pepper
1–2 tsps Dijon/English mustard

A little olive oil for frying
Tomato ketchup
Pesto (optional)
Mango chutney (optional)
Rocket/green leaves
Salad dressing (pg 187)

1. Preheat oven to 200°C/400°F/gas 6. Heat baguette till warmed through.
2. Beat seasoned eggs in a bowl. Add mustard and beat again. Make the omelette (pg 30). Slap it on a plate and roll it up.
3. Cut baguette lengthways, slather with ketchup/pesto/mango chutney.
4. Add the leaves and omelette and drizzle with the salad dressing.

Mozzarella, Tomato & Avocado

1 ciabatta roll, split
A little olive oil
1 clove garlic, cut in half (optional)
2 slices avocado
2 slices mozzarella
Thick slice tomato
Fresh basil
A little salt

1. Preheat oven to 200°C/400°F/gas 6. Rub a little oil onto the cut insides of the roll.
2. Rub with garlic. Layer avocado, cheese, tomato, basil. Season as you go. Heat till warm and cheese a bit melty.

YOU CAN

* skip the baking – enjoy cold
* make Mozzarella, Tomato & Basil Salad. Arrange sliced ingredients, overlapping, on a plate. Drizzle with dressing (pg 187). Add basil.

* make Italian Club Sandwich. Toast 3 bread slices. Remove crusts. Layer up with cheese, tomato, basil, rocket, dressing or a little mayo/pesto.

Sizzling Spicy Spuds in Pitta

Oil for griddling
2 cold cooked potatoes, cubed
1 clove garlic, crushed
1 tsp tandoori powder or turmeric/cumin mix
Salt and pepper
Squeeze lemon/ lime juice
Fresh coriander
1 pitta bread
Mango chutney
A little red onion, chopped
2 tbsps hummus (pg 55)
Celery, thinly sliced
25g/1oz Cheddar, grated
10g/½oz raisins

1. Heat griddle pan. Brush with oil. Coat potato cubes lightly with garlic and spices. Either griddle for 1–2 minutes per side, turning, till crisp and hot, or fry in olive oil, garlic and spices till done.
2. Season with salt, pepper, lemon juice, coriander. Warm pitta till puffy.
3. Split pitta along one side. Spread with mango chutney. Add everything else. Eat warm or cold.

YOU CAN

* fry up a little onion with garlic and spices as above. Add drained cooked chickpeas. Cook gently for 5 minutes. Tip into pitta with plain yogurt (pg 18) and extras.

Griddled Veg Panini

Veg selection
  Aubergine, sliced
  Courgette, sliced
  Red onion, quartered
  Red/orange pepper, de-seeded,
    quartered
  Butternut squash, peeled, sliced
  Olive oil
  Salt and black pepper
  Lemon juice (optional)
  Fresh herbs (basil, parsley,
    coriander)
  1 panini

1. Heat a griddle pan till very hot.
2. Brush vegetables with a little olive oil. Slap onto griddle (don't overcrowd it).
3. Turn veg when they colour/soften. Remove whenever they look done.
4. Season. Squeeze lemon juice, scatter herbs. Stuff into warmed/toasted panini.

YOU CAN
✳ layer in sliced mozzarella/grated Cheddar. Brush both sides of panini with a little oil, layer up and put on hot griddle/under grill for 5 minutes/till hot and cheese melting.
✳ dot cooked veg with goat's cheese and grill gently
✳ spread bread with hummus, tapenade or pesto

Courgette Fritter Pittas

  ½ x fritter batter (pg 59)
  2 courgettes
  Oil for frying
  Salt
  2 pitta breads
  Sweet chilli sauce
  Green salad leaves
  Tomato, sliced
  Mayo

1. Make half quantity of fritter batter.
2. Slice courgettes. Dunk into batter and fry (pg 59).
3. Drain on kitchen roll. Sprinkle salt.
4. Meantime, warm pittas till puffy. Split open.
5. Load with chilli sauce, fritters, salad, tomato, mayo.

YOU CAN
✳ griddle thin strips of courgette in oil, 2 mins per side. Add salt, squeeze of lemon/lime, a little chopped chilli, fresh herb. Spread cream cheese on baguette. Slap courgettes in.

Juicy Mushroom

  2 slices bread
  Mustard
  A few mushrooms, chopped
  A little olive oil
  Garlic, crushed or purée
  4 drops soy sauce/tamari

1. Spread bread slice with mustard.
2. Fry mushrooms in oil with crushed/purée garlic. Add soy sauce/tamari.
3. Pile onto bread. Sandwich it.

CLASSIC SARNIES

Great homemade bread – classic fillings – tasty homemade extras – adds up to sarnies you'll never get bored with.

Cream Cheese & Cucumber Pickle

2 slices white/brown bread
Cream cheese (pg 187)
Cucumber pickle (pg 185)

1. Spread one slice of bread with cheese.
2. Top with pickle and then second slice.

Old-Style Ploughman's

2 slices brown/white/soda
   bread (pg 97)
Apple chutney/Branston pickle
Mayo or half a ripe tomato
3–4 slices strong Cheddar/
   Lancashire cheese
Few rings red onion
3–4 thin slices tomato
1 stick celery, thinly sliced
Spinach leaves/watercress/
   iceberg/soft lettuce

1. Spread chutney/pickle over one slice of bread. Spread mayo or squeeze a tomato over the other.
2. Stack with rest of ingredients. Sandwich.

YOU CAN
* sub in hummus/grated carrot
* slice in some apple

Crunchy Celery

2 slices bread
Bit of butter
2 sticks celery, thinly sliced
Grated Cheddar
Dollop mayo
Apple chutney (optional)

1. Lightly butter the bread.
2. Mix celery, Cheddar, mayo.
3. Pile between bread spread with optional chutney.

Brie, Spinach, Cranberry, Grapes, Pinenuts

2 slices bread/focaccia/soda
   bread/ciabatta
Cranberry sauce/relish
Thinly sliced Brie
Mayo/garlic mayo
6 red/white grapes
Iceberg lettuce, shredded
Cucumber, thinly sliced, or
   cucumber pickle (pg 185)
Tomato, thinly sliced

1. Spread one bit of bread with cranberry. Top with Brie.
2. Spread second with mayo, grapes, salad, tomato. Sandwich together.

Egg Mayo, Chilli Jam & Green Leaf

2 slices bread/1 Cheese Fat
   Rascal (pg 95), split
1 hard-boiled egg (pg 13)
Dollop mayo
Salt and pepper
Chilli jam/sweet chilli sauce/
   apple chutney

1. Mash the egg with mayo, salt, pepper.
2. Spread relish on bread.
3. Top with egg mayo.

YOU CAN
* add spinach, rocket, cucumber, watercress
* finely chop tomato, mix into mayo

49

CHEESE SNACKS

The ultimate lunch – a slice or two of tasty cheese with homemade bread, chutney and a crisp bit of fruit, or try these – check cheese is veggie.

3 eggs
200ml/7fl oz milk
50g/2oz butter, melted
150g/5oz strong Cheddar, grated
4 spring onions, finely sliced
1 small red chilli, de-seeded, finely chopped
Fresh parsley/thyme/coriander
Grated Cheddar/Parmesan for topping

1. Preheat oven to 190°C/375°F/gas 5. Tip flour, baking powder, salt, sugar, cayenne, mustard into a bowl.
2. Whisk eggs and milk together. Add warm (not hot) melted butter. Add to flour mix with cheese, onion, chilli, herbs. Fold very lightly together (pg 10) into a lumpy batter, no beating.
3. Divide between 12 large muffin cases in a tin. Top with cheese. Bake 20–30 minutes or till well risen.

Welsh Rarebit

25g/1oz soft butter
110g/4oz strong Cheddar, grated
1 tsp English mustard
Shake Henderson's Relish
2 tbsps milk
Squeeze lemon juice
2 slices wholemeal/white/ Treacle Bread (pg 97)

1. Preheat grill. Mix all topping ingredients.
2. Toast one side of bread. Spread topping on the other.

3. Grill till melted and bubbling. Eat with fruit/salad.

YOU CAN
* top with poached eggs for Buck Rabbit
* mash into stuffed baked potatoes
* make more, keeps 1 week, chilled

Cheese & Chilli Lunch Muffins

275g/10oz plain flour, sifted
3 tsps baking powder
½ tsp salt
1 tbsp sugar
Good pinch cayenne
Pinch mustard powder

Grilled Cheese & Salad

1–2 slices white/wholemeal/ Treacle Bread (pg 97)
Smear mango/apple chutney
Strong hard cheese, e.g. Cheddar, Lancashire
Grated onion/apple (optional)

Salad
Watercress/spinach
1 pear/nectarine, sliced
Chicory (optional)
Dressing (pg 187)

1. Toast one side of bread under grill.
2. Smear untoasted side with chutney. Cover completely with sliced, crumbled or grated cheese mixed with grated options.
3. Grill till bubbling. Toss leaves and fruit in dressing.

YOU CAN
✳ top with a poached egg for Croque Madame

Croque Monsieur Toastie

2 slices white/brown bread
Butter
Mustard
Tomato, sliced
Cheese, sliced

1. Heat grill/sandwich toaster/griddle pan. Butter bread.
2. Smear mustard on one slice. Top with tomato, cheese, then second bread slice, buttered side down.
3. Grill, turning, till cooked through and toasted.

YOU CAN
✳ top with a poached or fried egg for Croque Madame

Speedy Pizza Bread

Baguette or ciabatta, sliced open
1 clove garlic, cut in half
Olive oil
2 tbsps passata/own tomato sauce (pg 106–107)
Pinch dried oregano
Cheddar/Gruyère, sliced/grated

1. Preheat oven to 230°C/450°F/gas 8.

2. Rub garlic over bread. Drizzle with a little olive oil. Bake on tray for 5 minutes.
3. Make a mix of passata/tomato sauce, crushed garlic, oregano. Spread over hot bread.
4. Top with cheese. Cook 5 minutes or till bubbling.

Tomato & Mozzarella Bruschetta

4 slices ciabatta/baguette
A little olive oil
1 clove garlic, cut
110g/4oz Mozzarella, thinly sliced
1–2 tomatoes, diced
Salt and pepper
Basil (optional)

Dressing
1 tsp olive oil
1 tsp red wine vinegar/lemon juice

1. Preheat oven to 200°C/400°F/gas 6.
2. Sit bread on tray. Drizzle a little oil. Bake till crisp (5–10 minutes).
3. Rub garlic over bread. Spread cheese to cover. Top with tomato, a few drops of olive oil, seasoning. Bake till just softening.
4. Add dressing, optional basil.

YOU CAN top baked bread with...
✳ hummus, tomato
✳ tomato, olive, basil dressing
✳ tapenade, cottage cheese
✳ cream cheese, cucumber
✳ guacamole, salsa

Guacamole
1 ripe avocado
½ clove garlic, crushed
1 tbsp olive oil
1 tbsp finely chopped coriander
1 tbsp lime juice
Salt and black pepper

Salsa
2 ripe tomatoes, finely chopped
½ small onion/shallot, finely chopped
1 clove garlic, crushed
½ small red/green chilli, de-seeded, chopped
Lime juice to taste
Bit of fresh coriander, chopped
Pinch caster sugar
Salt and black pepper

Tortillas (per person)
2 wheat tortillas
Grated Cheddar
1 small red onion/2 spring onions
½ red/green chilli, de-seeded, sliced

Quesadillas

Great Mexican-style street food. Get loads of flavours in there, then chop up and share round. Please the crowd when the money's running out.

1. Guacamole: scoop flesh out of avocado, down to the skin. Add garlic. Blitz or mash with a fork or bash with a pestle and mortar. Add oil, coriander, lime, seasoning to taste.

2. Salsa: mix everything together.

3. Tortilla wedges: heat a large frying pan without oil. Slap a tortilla down. Immediately sprinkle with cheese, onion, chilli, and top with second tortilla. Heat for 1 minute. Turn and heat for 1–2 minutes till cheese melts.

4. Cut into quarters. Serve with guacamole and salsa.

YOU CAN
* grate in some mozzarella cheese, add black beans, coriander or basil
* vegans – use re-fried beans instead of cheese
* add finely chopped chilli, red onion, tomato to guacamole
* sit avocado stone in bowl with guacamole and cover to stop browning
* grill tortilla for 1 minute. Cover with any pizza topping. Grill 2 minutes till bubbling.

Baked Feta, Tzatziki & Flatbreads

I fell in love with this on a post-A-level trip to Greece. Scoop up the cheese with easy cumin flatbreads.

1. Preheat oven to 200°C/400°F/gas 6. Sit feta on a foil square. Add tomatoes, herbs, lemon, oil. Scrunch foil edges together to seal in a loose parcel. Bake on a tray for 15 minutes or till melting while you prep extras.

2. Tzatziki: grate unpeeled cucumber. Blot moisture on kitchen paper/tea towel. Mix with yogurt, garlic, salt.

3. Flatbread: make dough (pg 54 steps 2–4). Roll out. Cook both sides till done but soft. Wrap in tea towel to keep warm.

4. Slap the cooked cheese parcel onto a plate. Unwrap. Scoop up with a flatbread, spoon on some tzatziki.

YOU CAN

✱ cube cheese and cook in parcels on the barbecue

✱ use several packs to bake in a big uncovered dish as above to feed more

1 x 200g/7oz pack feta
A few cherry tomatoes, quartered
Fresh basil/thyme/oregano or a pinch dried
Pinch smoked/plain paprika (optional)
Lemon juice
Olive oil

Tzatziki

15cm/6in length cucumber
175g/6oz creamy natural yogurt (Greek is best, or own (pg 18))
1–2 cloves garlic, crushed
Bit of sea salt

Cumin flatbread

1 x Turkish pizza dough (pg 54)

MAKES 8 **EXPRESS** **VEGAN OPT.**

Cumin flatbread dough
275g/9½oz plain white flour
1 tsp cumin seeds
225ml/8fl oz natural yogurt
Pinch salt

Topping
Cherry tomatoes
A little olive oil
Feta, crumbled
Coriander/parsley, chopped
Black olives, diced
A little red onion, sliced/chopped
Pinenuts
A little salt
Lemon to squeeze (optional)

Fast Turkish Pizzas with Feta

Fast cumin flatbreads make a perfect base for these tasty little beauties – or cook and leave plain to serve with hummus and other mezze.

1. Halve tomatoes. De-seed with a teaspoon. Prep toppings.

2. Make dough by mixing sifted flour, cumin, yogurt, salt. Roll into a ball. Sit on a floured surface. Divide into 8.

3. Roll out each portion on a lightly floured surface into a very thin circle. Preheat a frying pan and grill.

4. One portion at a time, lift carefully onto the dry hot pan. Cook 1–2 minutes till browned. (Turn, repeat a few seconds if plain for mezze.)

5. Remove. Sprinkle with topping and a little olive oil. Sit it under the grill on a baking tray for 2 minutes or till the bread crisps at the edge.

6. Eat open or folded with tzatziki, hummus, baba ganoush, tahini dip (opposite).

Baba Ganoush

1 large aubergine
1½ tbsps olive oil
1 clove garlic
1 small onion
Juice of ½ large lemon
Salt
Bit of parsley/coriander

1. Heat oven to 200°C/400°F/gas 6.
2. Bake whole aubergine for 20–30 minutes till black and soft.
3. Slice and scrape flesh out (discard skin). Blitz flesh with remaining ingredients. Season, taste and adjust. Chill. Eat with pitta/veg sticks.

YOU CAN

✳ blacken aubergine over a flame, under grill or on griddle
✳ add 2 tbsps yogurt, ½ tbsp tahini

Tahini Dip

150g/5oz tahini
4 cloves garlic, crushed
Juice 2 lemons
125ml/4fl oz warm water
**2 tbsps chopped coriander/
   parsley**
Salt

Blitz it all up with a handblender or in a processor.

YOU CAN

✳ add a pinch of cumin
✳ eat with Pitta Crisps. Cut pittas across horizontally. Brush with oil and paprika/salt or mix of crushed garlic and butter. Bake 10 minutes at 180°C/350°F/gas 4.

Hummus

1 x 400g/14oz can chickpeas
2 cloves garlic, crushed
Juice of 1 large lemon
1 tbsp tahini
Salt
**2 tbsps good olive oil, plus
   extra for drizzling**
2 tbsps water/chickpea liquid
Sprinkling of paprika (optional)
Fresh coriander (optional)
Pinenuts (optional)

1. Drain chickpeas, saving liquid.
2. Tip into a bowl or processor with garlic, lemon juice, tahini, salt.
3. Heat oil and water/chickpea liquid gently in a pan. Add to mix.

4. Blitz or mash with a fork. Add extra water to get it smoother.
5. Taste. Adjust with lemon, salt. Tip into bowl. Drizzle olive oil.
6. Sprinkle paprika, coriander, pinenuts. Eat warm as dip/spread or chill it.

YOU CAN

✳ add 1 tsp each cumin, chilli, ground coriander, honey
✳ blitz in caramelized onions (pg 132), roasted red pepper
✳ top with chickpeas
✳ stuff into a hollowed-out pepper for a box-to-go with bread/veg sticks/pitta
✳ cheat. Mash chickpeas with a bit of soy sauce, parsley, olive oil.

175g/6oz dried chickpeas
1 small onion (approx 50g/2oz),
   v finely chopped
2–3 fat cloves garlic, crushed
1½ tsps ground cumin
1 tsp ground coriander
1 tsp chilli powder or 1 small
   chopped, de-seeded chilli
2 tbsps fresh coriander
1–2 tbsps fresh parsley/mint, finely
   chopped and dried
Salt and pepper
1½ tbsps warm water
¾ tsp baking powder
Sunflower/vegetable oil for frying

Falafels

Team with hummus, dips, salads or stuff into pittas.

1. Soak dried chickpeas in double depth of water for minimum 12 hours. Drain. Dry v well. You want a dry mix.

2. Blitz in processor with onion, garlic, spices, herbs, seasoning.

3. Mix water, baking powder in cup. Stir into falafel mix.

4. Roll firmly into balls. Chill at least 30 minutes.

5. Tip 5cm/2in oil into frying pan/wok. When hot enough to crisp a breadcrumb, fry a few of the balls at a time, turning, till golden brown, cooked through. Sit on kitchen paper.

YOU CAN

✳ eat in wraps, cumin flatbread or slap in a lunch box

✳ bind with a bit of beaten egg if mix is dry. Or fry in breadcrumbs.

✳ eat with couscous (pg 133), bulgur (pg 13), quinoa salads

450g/1lb onions, halved, v thinly
    sliced, crescent-moon style
1 tsp salt
1 tsp cumin
1 tsp ground coriander
Handful fresh coriander, chopped
1 tsp turmeric
2 green chillies, de-seeded, v finely
    chopped
60g/2½oz gram (chickpea) flour
½ tsp baking powder
Sunflower/groundnut oil

Raita
Cucumber
Few tbsps yogurt (pg 18)
1 clove garlic, crushed

Onion Bhajis & Raita

Crunchier and lighter than most bhajis.

1. Make raita: peel and dice a length of cucumber. Mix with yogurt
and crushed garlic. Set aside.

2. Meantime, make bhajis: sprinkle onion slices with salt
in colander or sieve. Leave 30 minutes to draw out moisture.

3. Rinse onions under running water. Squeeze. Dry v well in tea
towel. Transfer to bowl.

4. Separately, mix salt, cumin, dried and fresh coriander, turmeric,
chillies, gram flour, baking powder. Mix in with onions.

5. Shape into bhajis: squeeze and roll into 12 balls.

6. Heat 8cm/3in oil in wok, deep saucepan or frying pan. When
hot enough to crisp a breadcrumb, fry 4 at a time, carefully turning
till cooked through, browned and golden. Drain on kitchen paper.

1 x 250g/9oz pack firm tofu
Sprinkling of fine salt
Sprinkling of pepper
Pinch sugar
Pinch five-spice powder
Plain flour
1 large egg
Dried breadcrumbs (pg 12) or panko
 (from Chinese/Asian shops)
Vegetable/groundnut oil for frying
Sweet chilli sauce for dipping

Salt & Pepper Tofu

Here's my favourite way with tofu – which can be bland to be honest. This one's crispy, spicy, soft inside and gorgeous – plus a top source of protein.

1. Prep tofu to remove excess moisture if you have time (pg 12).
2. Mix salt, pepper, sugar, five-spice and flour on a plate. Beat egg on another. Spread breadcrumbs over a third.
3. Blot the tofu dry. Cut into 16 cubes. Dip each into flour, egg, crumbs to cover. Heat enough oil in a deep pan or wok to deep-fry (at least 10cm/4in) until it will instantly crisp a breadcrumb.
4. Add a third of the cubes to fry for a little until they brown and crisp. Remove. Drain on kitchen paper and cook the remainder. Dip in sweet chilli sauce.

YOU CAN
✱ eat cubes on hot noodles/rice/salad
✱ dip into ginger drizzle (opposite) – try adding lime juice
✱ vegans – use soy sauce/milk mix instead of egg dip

Veggie Fritters with Ginger Drizzle

This could be one of the tastiest ways to eat vegetables. Batter seals in the flavour and protects the texture. Great to dip and share and deliciously moreish.

1. Mix dip ingredients. Prep veg. Heat enough oil for frying as for Salt & Pepper Tofu (opposite).

2. Make the batter: sift flour, salt, cayenne into a bowl. Gradually beat in the oil and water using a wooden spoon or balloon whisk.

3. When the frying oil is hot (190°C/375°F or hot enough to crisp a crumb), dunk a few veg into the batter to coat. Fry a few at a time for a few minutes, turning to brown them evenly. Drain on kitchen paper. Dip in ginger drizzle or sweet chilli sauce.

YOU CAN

* make Veg Tempura: briefly mix 75g/3oz plain flour, 1 tbsp corn or rice flour, pinch salt, 200ml/7fl oz chilled water into a lumpy batter with chopsticks. Cook as above.

* make Italian Cauliflower Fritters. Boil florets for 4 minutes. Drain. Coat in flour, pinch salt and cayenne. Dunk in a mix of beaten egg, grated Parmesan, salt, pepper, oregano. Shallow-fry in olive oil till cooked and crispy.

FEEDS 2–3 · VEGAN · EXPRESS

Dip
2 tsps grated fresh ginger
2 tbsps caster sugar
2 tbsps soy sauce
2 tbsps rice wine
4 tbsps rice wine vinegar

Veg
Courgettes, diagonally sliced
Onion rings
Cauliflower, blanched
Mushrooms, sliced or whole
Aubergine, sliced
Butternut squash, sliced

Batter
110g/4oz plain flour
Pinch salt
Pinch cayenne
1 tbsp olive oil
200ml/7fl oz water

Vegetable/groundut oil for frying

PER PERSON · VEGAN

1 fat baking potato
Oil (optional)
Butter/soy spread
Salt and pepper

Baked Spuds

Get hold of Maris Piper, King Edward, Rooster or other good floury potatoes.

1. Heat oven to 200°C/400°F/gas 6. Scrub spuds. Prick with a fork, or stick a metal skewer through. Rub skin with oil and salt for crisp skin, or wrap in foil, oil-free, for soft skin. Bake for 1 hour or till tender.

2. Cut, punch or squeeze open. Mash in butter/soy spread and seasoning. Add your choice of toppings.

YOU CAN

✱ top with Veggie Chilli (pg 120), Dahl (pg 129), Baked Beans, Chillied Chickpeas (pg 160), cheese and Guacamole (pg 52), Hummus (pg 55), Coleslaw (pg 73), cottage cheese, Tzatziki (pg 53), Cauliflower Cheese (pg 158), Ratatouille (pg 155), Garlic Mushrooms, Salsa (pg 52), Marmite, Waldorf Salad: nuts, raisins, apple, celery, dressing (pg 185–7)

✱ save skin. Brush with butter. Season. Add bit of cheese. Bake at 200°C/400°F/gas 6 for 10 minutes. Fill with any of above or dip in guacamole/salsa/other dip.

✱ microwave? Cook on full power one at at time 8–10 minutes. Hot!

✱ re-use cold baked spuds. Chop roughly. Bake in hot oven drizzled with olive oil, sliced garlic, herbs, till crunchy. Great with chutney/salad.

PER PERSON · VEGAN OPT.

Hot baked potato
Butter/soy spread
Salt and pepper
Mustard
Lemon juice
Cheddar
Any windowsill herb

Stuffed Baked Spuds

Great for a meal or make loads for parties. Note: wrap and freeze so they're there when you need them.

1. Cut freshly baked potato in half. Scoop flesh into a bowl. Put skin back into the oven to start crisping.

2. Mash flesh with butter/soy spread, salt, pepper, mustard, lemon juice, grated cheese and chopped herbs.
3. Pile back into seasoned half-shells. Top with more cheese. Bake for 10 minutes or till crisp and bubbling.

YOU CAN
* mash in 1–2 tbsps Rarebit mix (pg 50)
* for Leek and Cheese baked spuds, gently fry sliced leek in garlic and butter. Add to mix with Cheddar, garlic, cream cheese (omit for vegans).
* add gently fried garlic mushrooms

Tortilla

Perfect food to go – get a big slice and take it out with you. Eating in? Team it with a green or tomato salad.

FEEDS
3–4

110ml/4fl oz olive oil
3 large onions, thinly sliced
4 large potatoes, peeled, thinly sliced
8 large eggs
Salt and black pepper

1. Heat oil in a large frying pan. Add onions and potatoes. Cook gently for 20 minutes or till spuds are tender but holding shape. Tip into a bowl. Drain the oil off.
2. Beat eggs and seasoning. Add to the onions and potatoes.
3. Put 2 tablespoons oil back into the pan. Tip tortilla mix in. Lower the heat after a minute. Cook slowly till set. Run a spatula or knife round to loosen the edge. Flash under medium grill to finish.

YOU CAN
* slap a slice in a sarnie to go
* sandwich quarters together with cream

Filling
25g/1oz butter
2 handfuls baby spinach
Salt and pepper
Pinch nutmeg
2 tbsps tomato sauce (pg 106)/
  passata

Omelette
3 eggs
¼ tsp mustard
10g/½oz Cheddar, grated
Salt and pepper
Knob of butter

3-Egg Omelette with Spinach & Tomato Sauce

The secret of a good omelette … get it light, work fast and don't overcook it. Roll it out of the pan instead of lifting it.

1. **Filling:** melt butter in a pan over medium heat. Add spinach. Stir for 1 minute or until spinach wilts. Remove. Season with salt, pepper, nutmeg.
2. Warm tomato sauce in another pan.
3. **Omelette:** crack eggs into a bowl with mustard, cheese, seasoning and beat with a fork.
4. Heat a frying pan over high heat. Add the knob of butter.
5. When the pan is almost smoking, pour the egg mix in. Using a spatula or fork, pull the egg mix back on one side, tilting the runny mix back into its place. Continue till base is just set, top still liquid.
6. Add a line of tomato sauce topped with the spinach.
7. Roll omelette directly onto a warmed plate so it folds over onto itself.

YOU CAN fill with…
∗ grated cheeses and diced tomato
∗ crumbled goat's cheese, apple chutney, salad leaf
∗ mushroom and caramelized onion
∗ stir-fried spring onion, garlic, beansprouts, mushrooms, coriander, sugar, lime in sesame oil. Drizzle with teriyaki sauce.
∗ fried cubed potato and onion, cream cheese (pg 187), rocket

Courgette Frittata

Frittata is like a blank canvas for all your favourite flavours – chuck in whatever you fancy according to season.

FEEDS 2 EXPRESS

1 onion, thinly sliced
1 clove garlic, crushed
Olive oil
2–3 medium courgettes, thinly sliced
6 eggs
A little thyme, mint, oregano
Salt and pepper
Feta, crumbled, or Cheddar, grated

1. Fry onion and garlic gently in oil till soft, not coloured.
2. Add courgettes. Cook 5 minutes or till softening.
3. Beat the eggs with herbs and seasoning. Tip into the pan.
4. Cook on low heat for a few minutes until just set.
5. Sprinkle with cheese. Finish under the grill. Eat hot, warm, cold.

YOU CAN
* add a handful of cooked angel hair, linguine or spaghetti
* add tomato compôte. Skin, de-seed, chop 2 tomatoes. Simmer in 2 tbsps olive oil for 20 minutes. Season, add fresh basil. Stir in.
* use very finely sliced broccoli florets instead of courgettes
* add black olives. Stir in sour cream or cream cheese (pg 187).
* add cubed cooked sweet potatoes, potatoes, butternut squash, peppers
* if you're really skint – soak **1** thick slice crustless bread in **3** tbsps milk for **10** minutes. Squeeze dry. Beat in **3** eggs, season, add optional cheese, herbs. Fry. Eat hot or cold. Delicious.
* add left-over risotto

YESTERDAY'S PASTA AND RICE

Transform extra cooked pasta and rice into cheap, tasty lunches.

FEEDS 1 · **VEGAN OPT.** · **EXPRESS**

Option One
Rigatoni, cooked
Tomato sauce (pg 106)/passata
 mixed with garlic
Mozzarella

Option Two
Penne, cooked
Crème fraîche
Dijon mustard
Gruyère cheese
Breadcrumbs
Garlic
Butter/olive oil

Option Three
Penne, cooked
Chickpeas
Tomato sauce (pg 106)/passata
 mixed with garlic
Grated Cheddar

Freestyle Baked Pasta

Baked pasta three ways – vary your pasta shapes and extras.

1. Butter or oil ovenproof dishes. Heat oven to 190°C/375°F/gas 5.

2. Option one: mix rigatoni with tomato sauce. Spoon into dish. Cover with mozzarella.

3. Option two: mix crème fraîche, mustard, cheese. Stir into penne. Top with a mix of blitzed breadcrumbs with garlic (pg 10, 12). Dot with butter or drizzle with oil.

4. Option three: stir penne and chickpeas into tomato sauce. Top with grated Cheddar.

5. Bake for 20 minutes or cook under the grill till hot and bubbling.

Freestyle Pasta Salad

Multitasks as a quick snack or salad to-go, or to eat in.

FEEDS 2 · VEGAN OPT. · EXPRESS

Cooked pasta, e.g. penne, fusilli
Dressing (pg 185–7)
Fresh herbs

Extras

Red onion, spring onion, cheese, roasted peppers (pg 71), hard boiled egg, chickpeas/butterbeans/cannellini, baby potatoes, spinach, watercress, tomatoes, olives, green/broad/soya beans, griddled halloumi, sundried tomatoes, croûtons

1. Mix a little dressing with cooked pasta while still warm. Cool. Cover. Chill. Return to room temperature next day.

2. Add more dressing and herbs. Enjoy on its own or with green salad and extras.

Stir-Fried Rice & Ginger Drizzle

Tasty way to boost vitamin B (builds brain cells). Vary veg. Vegans – use silken tofu to bind it.

FEEDS 1 · EXPRESS

200g/7oz chilled cooked basmati/long-grain rice (or cook 75g/3oz dried)
50g/2oz frozen peas
2 eggs
1 spring onion, chopped
2 tbsps veg/sunflower/groundnut oil
Dash sesame oil
A few asparagus tips, cooked 2 minutes (optional)
Fresh coriander (optional)
Salt and pepper
Ginger Drizzle (pg 59)

1. Fetch rice or cook fresh. Pour boiling water over peas to defrost.

2. Beat eggs. Add half spring onion.

3. Heat wok. Add oils. Reduce heat.

4. Add egg. Stir till starting to scramble. Add rice. Increase heat.

5. Mix with fork, adding vegetables, herb, seasoning, till hot.

6. Tip into bowl. Add ginger drizzle/chilli sauce/ketchup/soy.

YOU CAN

✱ make Rice Salad. Drizzle olive oil and lemon juice over warm cooked rice. Cool. Add cooled cooked peas/broad beans/fresh herbs/cherry tomatoes.

SALADS – MAINS & SIDES
A mix of fresh ideas and mainstream classics.

A few new/waxy salad potatoes
Salad dressing (pg 187)
Green beans
Salt and pepper
A few croûtons (pg 11)
Lettuce/other leaves
A few black/green olives
Cherry tomatoes, halved
Cucumber, diced
Roast peppers (pg 71), cut into chunks
Red onion, sliced
1 hard-boiled egg (pg 13)

Freestyle Salad Niçoise

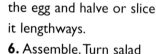

Makes a solid yet refreshing main course. For a lighter plate, skip the potatoes, but feel free to customize.

1. Boil potatoes in lightly salted water until just tender.
2. Meantime, make the dressing (pg 187).
3. Cook beans in boiling salted water till just tender. Rinse in cold water to refresh and retain colour.
4. Drain potatoes. Leave small ones whole – slice larger ones. Toss in a little dressing and season while still warm.
5. Make the croûtons. Prep salad leaves and veg. Peel shell from the egg and halve or slice it lengthways.
6. Assemble. Turn salad leaves in a little dressing. Present in layers – potato and leaves at the base – or tumble everything together.

YOU CAN
＊ add capers or pinenuts
＊ make Pan Bagnat – brush insides of a split baguette with garlicky olive oil. Layer in any of salad ingredients. Wrap in clingfilm. Squash with weights for 30 mins.

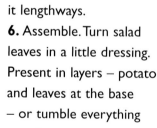

Tofu Salad

This salad's got it all. It's fresh and full of clean flavours that complement the tofu brilliantly and to top it off, it's incredibly healthy.

1. Prep tofu (pg 12) if time or just cut into 16 cubes. Mix marinade.
2. Turn tofu in the mix. Leave for five minutes or longer.
3. Prep salad ingredients and dressing.
4. Fry tofu pieces in a pan in a little vegetable and sesame oil, turning till browned all over. Pile salad onto plate. Top with tofu. Dress it.

YOU CAN

✱ coat cooked soba noodles in a little dressing. Add to the salad.

✱ fry tofu before sitting it in marinade. Leave. Thread on skewers. Brush with oil. Grill, turning till crisp. Eat with rice, stir-fry.

FEEDS 2 VEGAN OPT. EXPRESS

1 pack firm tofu
Vegetable and sesame oils for frying

Marinade
1 tbsp honey
1 tbsp soy sauce
1 tbsp hoisin sauce
½ tsp sesame oil
A little grated ginger (optional)

Salad
Handful beansprouts
Cucumber, cut into strips
Spinach/rocket
Spring onions
Peanuts, crushed/sesame seeds

Oriental dressing (pg 185)

Honey Mustard Dressing (pg 187)
A few crushed walnuts

Cheese discs
Plain flour
Salt and pepper
1–2 eggs
Fresh or dried breadcrumbs (pg 12)
4 thick slices goat's cheese
Vegetable oil for frying

Salad
Any green leaves
2 cooked beetroots, diced
1 orange sliced

Deep-Fried Goat's Cheese Salad

A perfect dinner party piece contrasting rich goat's cheese with piquant beetroot. Note: beetroot's a superfood (folate, minerals, vitamins). Stir-fry or steam the leaves for useful iron.

1. Make the dressing. Stir in crushed walnuts. Set aside.

2. Spread seasoned flour on a plate. Beat eggs on another. Spread breadcrumbs onto a third. Dip the cheese to cover into flour, egg, crumbs.

3. Chill or fry immediately in oil that's deep enough to cover the discs and hot enough to crisp a crumb immediately. Fry till golden.

4. Sit on dressed green leaves with beetroot, orange.

YOU CAN
* roast salted unpeeled beetroot in foil for 40 minutes or boil till tender
* grill uncrumbed cheese on foil or grill on toasted bread/croûtons

Big Mexican Salad

A crowd-pleasing mix of healthy bits (black beans and avocado for protein), salad, tortilla chips. Slap it onto the table for parties.

1. Combine all the salad ingredients together in a big bowl.
2. Make the dressing: crush garlic with a little salt, then whisk with other ingredients.
3. Pour over the salad and serve with sour cream/garlic yogurt.

YOU CAN
* use kidney beans
* add hard-boiled egg and fresh coriander
* add finely chopped red chilli or flakes to the dressing
* add fried onion rings (pg 161)

FEEDS 2–3   VEGAN OPT.   EXPRESS

Salad
¼ iceberg lettuce, torn into strips
110g/4oz tinned black beans
75g/3oz sweetcorn
10 cherry tomatoes, cut in half
½ red onion, finely sliced
1 avocado, sliced
75g/3oz Cheddar, grated
Handful tortilla chips

Dressing
1 clove garlic
Salt
4 tbsps olive oil
1 tbsp balsamic vinegar
2 tsps honey
Slurp tomato ketchup

To serve
Sour cream/garlic yogurt

69

FEEDS 2–3 **VEGAN**

225g/8oz puy lentils
850ml/1½ pints water/veg stock
4–6 spring onions, sliced
1 medium red onion, finely chopped
Handful cherry tomatoes or 4 large
    tomatoes, chopped
Freshly chopped parsley/mint/
    coriander/basil
Salt and pepper

Dressing

1 tsp caster sugar/honey
1 tsp mustard
1 tbsp any wine vinegar
5 tbsps good olive oil

FEEDS 2–3 **VEGAN OPT.**

Croûtons (pg 13)
1 butternut squash
Olive oil
3–4 cloves garlic, chopped
1 tsp cumin
Sprinkle chilli flakes

Choices

Cherry or other tomatoes
Avocado, diced
Cooked Puy lentils (pg 13)
Cooked black beans
Spinach/watercress/rocket
Any cheese, cubed
Goats cheese, crumbled
Red onion, sliced
Cucumber, diced
1 red onion, peeled
Olives
Roast beetroot
Dressing of choice (pg 185–7)

A Proper Lentil Salad

Puy lentils play well in salads. They keep a neat shape and absorb flavours brilliantly.

1. Wash lentils, checking for stones. Add to a pan with twice their volume of water or vegetable stock. Boil then simmer for 15–20 minutes till cooked, with a bit of bite.

2. Drain. Tip into a bowl. Whisk dressing ingredients together or shake in a jar.

3. Add salad bits to lentils. Pour dressing over and mix. Cool.

YOU CAN

✱ add hard-boiled egg, mozzarella, feta, olives, sundried tomatoes
✱ use other lentils, cook for less time

Butternut Squash Salad

A big hearty salad – with seasonal options. Shove in your favourite stuff and enjoy it.

1. Preheat oven 200°C/400°F/gas 6. Make croûtons (pg 13).

2. Cut squash lengthways. Remove seeds and pith. Chop into bite size chunks. Roll in olive oil.

3. Tip onto a baking tray. Scatter garlic, cumin, chilli.

4. Roast for 20 minutes or till soft. Scatter onto plates.

5. Add choice of extras. Drizzle olive oil or a dressing.

Roasted Red Pepper & Polenta

Classic hot 'n' cold salad combo.

1. For polenta: boil salted water. Add polenta in a steady stream, beating. Simmer on reduced heat, stirring (it sputters), for 5 minutes. Beat in butter, herbs.

2. Pour into a lightly-oiled shallow tin. Cool for 30 minutes.

3. For peppers: preheat oven to 230°C/450°F/gas 8. Bake on a tray for 30 minutes until blistered. Tip into a plastic bag for 15 minutes. Peel the skin away and remove seeds. Cut into strips. Season. Dress with oil and lemon.

4. Heat an oiled griddle pan. Slice polenta into triangles and slap on the pan. Leave until well marked. Turn to cook the other side. Pile mix of salad and peppers onto a plate. Top with polenta.

YOU CAN

∗ flavour-up polenta with 50g/2oz grated Parmesan added with butter

∗ add a few chilli flakes

∗ serve polenta with griddled veg (pg 48) or mushrooms (pg 26)

∗ use peppers in pasta dishes and other salads

Polenta
½ tsp salt
1.2 litres/2 pints of water
200g/7oz fast-cook polenta
50g/2oz butter
A bit of chopped sage or rosemary (optional)

Red pepper salad
4 red peppers
3tbsp olive oil
½ lemon, juiced
Salt and black pepper
Selection of leaves
Cherry tomatoes

Couscous Salad

Flavour it up and pile it high – couscous makes a speedy base for this sweet salad.

1. Mix all ingredients for the dressing. Set aside.

2. Meantime, cook the couscous (pg 133). Set aside.

3. Mix dressing into couscous. Eat with halloumi (pg 72), veg skewers (pg 137), hard-boiled or poached eggs, crumbled feta.

YOU CAN

∗ use any oil-based dressing (pg 185–7). Mix in chopped tomato, cucumber, spring onion, peppers, olives.

∗ stir in cooked beans or chickpeas, Puy lentils

∗ use mix to stuff peppers/tomatoes

300ml/½ pint boiling water
225g/8oz couscous

Dressing
50ml/2fl oz olive oil
2 tbsps lemon juice
2 tsps harissa
Lemon rind
2 tbsps parsley/coriander
25g/1oz raisins, chopped
25g/1oz dried apricot, chopped
Salt and pepper

Good Old Potato Salad

700g/1½lb potatoes
2 tbsps mayo
2 tbsps yogurt
1 clove garlic, crushed
Squeeze lemon juice
Salt and black pepper

Extras

Sliced red onion, gherkins,
cherry tomatoes, herbs

1. Cook spuds as East Meets West
Potato Salad (below). Cool.
2. Mix remaining ingredients. Stir
together. Top with extras.

East Meets West Potato Salad

700g/1½lb potatoes, peeled, or
new, unpeeled, in chunks
4 tbsps mayo
1 tbsp Chinese wine vinegar
2 drops sesame oil
1 clove garlic, crushed
1–2 tsps horseradish
Squeeze lemon
Fresh coriander/parsley
Salt and pepper
4 spring onions, sliced
6 radishes, sliced
Cucumber, sliced, quartered
Cress

1. Boil potatoes in lightly salted water
till just tender. Drain.
2. Mix mayo, vinegar, oil, garlic,
horseradish, lemon, herbs, seasoning.
Add spring onions. Stir into warm
potatoes.
3. Turn radishes, cucumber into mix
so still visible. Top with cress.

Tomato & Onion

Any ripe tomatoes or a mix
Red onion/shallots, sliced
Salt and pepper
Sugar
Salad dressing (pg 187)
Fresh parsley, basil, oregano,
marjoram, mint

1. Slice or chop tomatoes as you like.
Sprinkle with salt, pepper, sugar.
2. Scatter herbs on top. Drizzle
dressing or mix of vinegar and oil.

YOU CAN
✱ add sliced mozzarella and/or
avocado or cucumber

Chickpea & Parsley

1 x 400g/14oz can chickpeas
Olive oil
Salt and pepper
½ red onion, diced
1 clove garlic, diced (optional)
Fresh parsley
Lemon juice

1. Heat chickpeas in their water.
Drain well. Tip into a bowl.
2. Drizzle with olive oil and season.
3. Mix in onion, garlic, parsley.
4. Add lemon. Taste. Adjust.

YOU CAN
✱ use beans instead of chickpeas

Chilli Lime Halloumi

1 x 250g/9oz pack halloumi
Spinach/rocket/lettuce
Salad dressing (pg 187)
1 lime

1 red chilli, de-seeded, finely
chopped

1. Slice cheese thickly. Put salad into a
bowl. Toss in dressing.
2. Heat griddle or frying pan. Line
pan with foil if grilling. Slap slices of
cheese to fry/grill 1–2 minutes per
side till golden.
3. Drizzle with lime, chilli. Stack on
dressed salad.

YOU CAN
✱ marinate chunks of halloumi in
lime/garlic/oil. Skewer up with veg.
Grill and turn till melting.

Greek Salad

200g/7oz feta cheese
2–3 tbsps olive oil
Windowsill herbs: basil,
coriander, thyme, dill
4 large ripe tomatoes
½ cucumber
1 red onion
A few black olives
Lemon juice

1. Cube the feta. Turn in a bit of the
oil and herbs.
2. Chop tomatoes and cucumber.
Slice or dice the onion. Stick into a
bowl with olives and remaining herbs.

3. Drizzle remaining oil and lemon. Top with feta.

YOU CAN

* tip into a warm pitta with Hummus (pg 55), yogurt (pg 18), Tzatziki (pg 53)
* scoop with cumin flatbreads (pg 53)
* add chunks of watermelon

Coleslaw

½ head white cabbage
1 carrot
½ red onion, finely sliced
2 spring onions, finely sliced
175ml/6fl oz mayo
25ml/1fl oz Dijon mustard
1 dsp cider vinegar
Juice of ½ lemon
Pinch sugar
Couple of drops Tabasco
Salt and pepper

1. Finely shred cabbage and carrot (or grate it). Finely slice onions.
2. Combine rest of ingredients. Taste.
3. Mix everything together.

YOU CAN

* use French dressing instead of mayo
* use red cabbage instead of white
* add chopped dates, apple, orange, seeds, parsley

Caesar Salad

1 cos lettuce
Croûtons (pg 13)
½ tbsp capers, drained
Parmesan cheese

Dressing
2 egg yolks
1 tbsp Henderson's Relish
½ tbsp Tabasco
1 fat clove garlic, crushed
150ml/5fl oz light olive oil
Good squeeze lemon juice
Salt and black pepper
1–2 tbsps water

1. Wash lettuce. Blot dry. Tear into bits.
2. Make dressing: mix egg yolks, relish, Tabasco, garlic in a bowl. Beat oil in very slowly till the mixture is thick. Add juice. Taste. Season. Thin with water if desired.
3. Toss leaves in half the dressing.
4. Place in a bowl with croûtons, capers, shaved or grated cheese, rest of dressing.
5. Top with croûtons, cheese curls.

YOU CAN

* add chopped avocado, pinenuts

Bulgur Wheat Salad

110g/4oz bulgur wheat
600ml/1 pint boiling water
2–3 tbsps extra virgin
Olive oil
Juice of ½– 1 lemon
Salt and pepper
1 clove garlic, chopped
Handful mint, finely chopped
Handful parsley, finely chopped
3 tomatoes, diced small
Length of cucumber, diced small
1 red onion, diced small

1 pomegranate or seeds

1. Prep bulgar wheat (pg 13). Prep other ingredients.
2. Mix everything in a bowl. Season. Drizzle with oil and lemon.
3. Eat alone with mezze, flatbreads, tzatziki, or top with crumbled cheese.

YOU CAN

* use chopped dates, seeds, chopped orange instead of salad
* no fresh herbs? Toss in chopped rocket, watercress or baby spinach.
* use as a base for griddled veg or vegetable skewers
* chuck in a box for healthy to-go salad
* add beetroot and rocket

Panzanella

1 ciabatta or small crusty loaf
2 tbsps olive oil, extra for cooking
A little fresh basil/parsley
4 large fat tomatoes, chopped
½ cucumber, peeled, cubed
1 small red onion, chopped
1 clove garlic, sliced
1 tbsp red wine vinegar
Pinch sugar
Salt and pepper

1. Preheat oven to 200°C/400°F/gas 6.
2. Cut bread into rough chunks. Roll in oil.
3. Bake till golden (5–10 minutes).
4. Tip salad ingredients into a bowl. Add warm bread. Drizzle oil and vinegar.
5. Season and stir. Stand for 10 minutes. Eat.

AFTERNOON TEA

225g/8oz soft butter
200g/7oz brown sugar
175g/6oz caster sugar
2 eggs, beaten
1 tsp orange juice
½ tsp vanilla extract
350g/12oz plain white flour
1 level tsp bicarbonate of soda
Pinch salt
Grated rind of 1–2 oranges
110g/4oz chocolate chips/bits
A few raisins, chopped

House Fridge Chocolate-Chip Cookies

Slice up the dough and bake now or chill in the fridge for quick cookies anytime you want or when mates drop in.

1. Tip butter and sugars into a bowl. Cream till white and fluffy (pg 10).

2. Beat the eggs in, a bit at time. Add a pinch of flour if mixture splits. Add juice, vanilla. Fold in flour, bicarb, salt, rind. Add choc chips and raisins.

3. Sit dough on a lightly floured board. Roll into a thick sausage the diameter of a cookie. Lay the roll on baking paper. Wrap round to enclose and seal like a cracker. Chill for at least 1 hour.

4. Slice number of cookies you want off the roll, 1cm/½in thick. Remove paper. Place well apart on greased trays – they will spread. Bake at 180°C/350°F/gas 4 for 10 minutes or until golden brown.

5. Remove. Cool on the tray for 4 minutes to crisp. Dough lasts 2 weeks.

YOU CAN
* add chopped sour or glacé cherries, cinnamon, nuts, white chocolate chips

Ginger Chilli Hits

Seem to be the only thing my sister Poll ever cooks when she's at home, but I still love them.

1. Preheat oven to 190°C/375°F/gas 5.

2. Sift flour, bicarbonate, ginger into bowl. Add chilli and butter.

3. Rub lightly together between your fingertips to amalgamate. Fork in sugar, syrup, and mix to a soft dough. Roll into 14 balls.

4. Sit well apart on greased trays (they spread). Flatten slightly.

5. Bake 15–20 minutes till golden (watch – they burn easily). Crisp and cool on trays. Remove with a spatula.

YOU CAN
* use caster sugar for a softer finish, add grated orange rind
* top cooled biscuits with melted chocolate

MAKES 14 · **VEGAN OPT.** · **EXPRESS**

110g/4oz self-raising flour
1 tsp bicarbonate of soda
2 tsps ground ginger
A very few chilli flakes
50g/2oz butter, in bits
40g/1½oz demerara sugar
2 tbsps golden syrup

Top Chocolate Biscuits

Taste as good as they look. Perfect for a tea party.

1. Preheat oven to 190°C/375°F/gas 5. Cream butter and sugar together till light, white (pg 10). Beat the egg in gradually. Add vanilla.

2. Add sifted flour and semolina. Mix with a fork. Pull dough into a smooth ball. Roll it out thinly (3mm/one-eighth in) on a lightly floured surface. Cut into rounds with a cutter/glass.

3. Bake on a greased tray for 10 minutes or till just coloured. Cool for 3 minutes. Use a spatula to slide onto a rack. Melt chocolate (pg 12) or mix icing. Top using a teaspoon. Eat when set.

MAKES 10

110g/4oz soft butter
110g/4oz caster sugar
1 medium egg, well beaten
5 drops vanilla extract
250g/9oz plain white flour, sifted
25g/1oz semolina/polenta

Choc top
200g/7oz chocolate

Icing top
200g/7oz icing sugar (sifted)
Lemon juice

MAKES 12 **VEGAN OPT.**

175g/6oz butter
175g/6oz brown sugar
3 drops vanilla extract
200g/7oz self-raising flour
Pinch baking powder
175g/6oz oats
½ jar raspberry or other jam

Jammy Flapjacks

You've got oats for energy and jam for luxury. Eat in for tea or take to a mate's house. Grab one for breakfast with a smoothie or use as a sports bar.

1. Preheat oven to 180°C/350°F/gas 4. Grease a 18x30.5x4cm/ 7x12x1½in tin.

2. Cream butter and sugar (pg 10). Mix in vanilla, flour, baking powder, oats.

3. Tip half the mix into the tin, pressing to cover the base. Spread with jam. Top evenly with remaining mix.

4. Bake 20 minutes, till just golden. Remove. Mark into squares after 10 minutes. Remove from tin when cold.

YOU CAN

✳ make Choc Peanut Butter Flapjacks: mix 110g/4oz melted butter, 2½ tbsps golden syrup, ½ tbsp peanut butter, 75g/3oz brown sugar, 275g/10oz oats. Bake at 190°C/375°F/gas 5 for 15–25 minutes. Melt chocolate (pg 12) to top.

✳ make Crisp Fast-Track Flapjacks. Mix 110g/4oz oats, 10g/½oz semolina, 75g/3oz soft brown sugar, 110g/4oz melted butter. Press into a 28x18cm/ 11x7in tin. Bake 15 minutes at 190°C/375°F/gas 5. Mark into 12 when slightly cooled. Remove with spatula when cold.

Monster Meringues

Dunk the bowl and whisk-heads in boiling water to get them grease-free so the mix works. Dry well.

MAKES
6

Whites of 5 large eggs separated
   from yolks (pg 11)
275g/10oz caster sugar

1. Preheat oven to 150°C/300°F/gas 2. Grease then line a baking tray with greaseproof paper. Wash your hands.
2. Whisk egg whites in a large bowl till just stiffening (not dry).
3. Add sugar 1 tbsp at a time, whisking until nearly solid.
4. Create big blobs of mix well apart on the tin. Reduce heat to 140°C/275°F/gas 1. Cook 1½ hours. Switch oven off but leave meringues in for 1 hour to dry out. Peel paper off carefully. Eat singly or sandwich together with cream/buttercream.

YOU CAN

* bake one big layer for 1½ hours. Top with cream and fruit for Pavlova.
* add 1 tbsp sifted cocoa at end of step 3 or dip meringues in melted chocolate
* core 4 apples. Score line around their middles. Stuff with sugar/dates/orange juice/rum/ butter. Bake at 180°C/350°F/gas 4 for 45 minutes or till soft. Strip off top skin. Pile meringue on top. Bake for another 15–30 minutes.
* use egg yolks for mayo (pg 186)

MAKES 10

EXPRESS

200g/8oz self-raising flour
110g/4oz butter
75g/3oz caster sugar
110g/4oz mixed dried fruit
1 egg, beaten
1 tbsp milk

Good Old Rock Cakes

Simple as you can get, with a great taste and in spite of the name, un-rock like.

1. Preheat oven to 200°C/400°F/gas 6. Grease a baking tray.
2. Sift flour into a bowl. Rub in butter using your fingertips (pg 10).
3. Add sugar, fruit, beaten egg and milk. Mix to a stiff dough.
4. Place 10 rocky piles of mix well apart on the tray. Bake 15–20 minutes or till cooked through. Cool on rack.

YOU CAN
* add chopped glacé cherries, mixed spice
* add ½–1 tsp cinnamon at step 2. Omit fruit. Roll into 10 balls. Make a hole with finger/teaspoon. Add jam. Pinch hole closed. Sprinkle sugar. Bake 10 minutes at 220°C/425°F/gas 7.

Cherry Fat Rascals

Another Yorkshire classic. My dad can't resist them and I don't blame him. They taste buttery and gorgeous.

1. Preheat oven to 200°C/400°F/gas 6. Grease baking trays.

2. Sift flours, baking powder, salt into a bowl. Rub butter into the mix (pg 10). Stir in sugar, rinds, spices, currants, chopped cherries.

3. Beat the egg and milk together. Mix in with a fork for a soft stiff dough (not too sticky). Knead lightly into a ball.

4. Roll out on a floured surface till 2cm/¾in thick. Cut out with a 9cm/3½in cutter or use saucers to trace 5 or 6 rascals.

5. Sit well apart on trays. Top with whole cherries, almonds if using. Brush with glaze. Bake 20 minutes. Eat warm/cold with butter.

YOU CAN
∗ add choc chips at step 3 with more orange rind

150g/5oz plain flour
150g/5oz self-raising flour
1 tsp baking powder
Pinch salt
150g/5oz butter
100g/3½oz caster sugar
Grated rind of 1 lemon
Grated rind of ½ orange
Big pinch ground nutmeg
¾ tsp ground cinnamon
2 handfuls currants
A few glacé cherries, chopped
1 egg
50ml/2fl oz milk
A few glacé cherries, whole
A few almonds (optional)

Glaze
1 egg yolk mixed with a little water

50g/2oz dark chocolate
6 drops vanilla extract
110g/4oz soft butter
225g/8oz soft brown sugar
2 eggs, beaten
50g/2oz plain flour
Pinch salt
½ tsp baking powder
225g/8oz walnuts/pecans
Grated rind of ½ large orange

Brownies

Classic US-style brownies. Sub in some raisins or cherries if you fancy.

1. Preheat oven to 190°C/375°F/gas 5. Grease and line base of a 20cm/8in square brownie tin.

2. Melt chocolate in a bowl over a pan of simmering water (pg 12). Add vanilla.

3. Beat butter and sugar together with wooden spoon till very light and creamy. Beat eggs in (add a pinch of flour if mix splits). Sift in flour, salt, baking powder. Beat well. Add nuts, rind.

4. Pour into tin. Level gently. Bake 35–40 minutes, till tester comes out clean (pg 91). Mark into squares after 15 minutes. Cool. Remove.

YOU CAN

✻ forget cooking – make Tiffin. Crush 200g/7oz chocolate digestives, 50g/2oz digestives. Add 110g/4oz raisins, 110g/4oz cherries. Melt 110g/4oz butter, 10g/½oz sugar, 4 tbsps golden syrup, cocoa. Add to mix. Press into 18x30.5x4cm/7x12x1½in tin. Set in fridge. Cut into 12.

Chocolate Truffle Bars

Like brownies but without the nuts, these bars are a bit sinful. Eat plain or ice patterns or messages.

MAKES 8

1. Preheat oven to 180°C/350°F/gas 4. Line a 20cm/8in square tin with baking paper. Sit a bowl over a pan of gently simmering water.
2. Break chocolate up. Tip it into bowl with butter. Allow to melt slowly, then stir together. Remove bowl from the heat.
3. Beat in the sugar and vanilla. Whisk all the eggs in vigorously.
4. Sift in flour and salt. Beat thoroughly. Tip truffle mix into the tin.
5. Cook for 35 minutes. Test (pg 91). It should still be a bit moist.
6. Remove. Cool in tin, marking into bars after 10 minutes.

200g/7oz dark chocolate
150g/5oz butter
225g/8oz caster sugar
2 tsps vanilla extract
2 large eggs
1 extra egg yolk
75g/3oz plain flour
Pinch salt

Optional icing
6 tbsps sifted icing sugar
A few drops water

200g/7oz plain white flour
25g/1oz cocoa
2 tsps baking powder
½ tsp bicarbonate of soda
2 eggs
75g/3oz caster sugar
2 tbsps sunflower oil
Grated rind of ½–1 orange
150ml/5fl oz milk
1 tbsp orange juice
110g/4oz choc chips/bits

Chocolate Muffins

You can't beat one of these with a cup of coffee, American-style.

1. Preheat oven to 200°C/400°F/gas 6. Grease holes in tray or line with muffin cases. Sift flour, cocoa, baking powder, bicarb into a bowl.

2. Beat eggs, sugar, oil, rind, milk, juice together. Mix into flour with a fork for a lumpy batter. Add chocolate bits. Spoon into cases.

3. Bake 15–20 minutes till risen, cooked through.

YOU CAN

✱ top with crumble. Rub 40g/1½oz flour, 20g/¾oz granulated sugar, 25g/1oz butter together. Sprinkle on muffin tops and bake.

✱ make Blueberry Muffins. Use 225g/8oz flour, lemon rind and juice, 2 tbsps poppy seeds and 110g/4oz fresh blueberries. Skip cocoa and choc chips.

Brunch Muffins

Bake a muffin or two from the basic mix whenever you fancy. It lasts a fortnight in the fridge. Customize to suit your mood.

1. Beat eggs, oil, vanilla, sugar, milk in a bowl.
2. Sift flours, salt, bicarb into another, adding oatmeal or bran, dates, dried fruit.
3. Beat liquid ingredients into dry ones, leaving lumps. Tip into plastic container with lid.
4. Preheat oven to 180°C/350°F/gas 4. Customize: put a little mix into a small bowl and add some extras. Or leave as is.
6. Spoon into muffin cases. Bake 15–20 minutes.

MAKES
12

2 large eggs
125ml/4fl oz sunflower/vegetable oil
1 tsp vanilla extract
175g/6oz dark brown sugar
500ml/17fl oz milk
110g/4oz plain wholemeal flour
175g/6oz plain white flour
Pinch salt
2 tsps bicarbonate of soda
110g/4oz medium oatmeal with bran (Mornflake) or wheat bran
110g/4oz dates, snipped
110g/4oz raisins/mixed fruit

Extras
Blueberries, diced apple, mashed banana, choc chips, cinnamon, nuts, seeds, fresh berries, cheese, grated carrot/courgette

Cinnamon Apple Muffins

Best Autumn option. Keep the batter lumpy for a better texture.

1. Preheat oven to 200°C/400°F/gas 6. Grease holes in muffin tin or line with cases.
2. Sift flour into a bowl. Add the dry ingredients and lemon rind. Make a well in the centre.
3. Mix milk, oil, eggs and essence. Tip, with apple, into well. Stir roughly for a lumpy batter. Fill almost to top of holes/cases. Sprinkle sugar.
4. Bake 20–25 minutes.

YOU CAN
✳ add fresh berries, dates, muesli
✳ spoon jam/marmalade into centre
✳ top with lemon icing (pg 87) or cream-cheese icing (pg 89). Add crumble.

MAKES
12

275g/10oz plain flour
1 tbsp baking powder
½ tsp cinnamon
½ tsp salt
175g/6oz polenta
150g/5oz caster sugar
Grated rind of 1 lemon
350ml/12fl oz milk
175ml/6oz sunflower oil
4 eggs, beaten
½ tsp almond/vanilla extract
1 large eating apple, diced
Demerara/granulated sugar

**MAKES
1**

175g/6oz soft butter
175g/6oz caster sugar
2 eggs, beaten
175g/6oz self-raising flour
Grated rind of 1 lemon
4 tbsps milk
1 tbsp lemon juice

Glaze
2–3 tbsps icing sugar, sifted
Juice of 1 lemon

Lemon Drizzle Cake

Intense flavour, beautiful texture and self-indulgence.
Always a good combination in my book.

1. Preheat oven to 160°C/320°F/gas 3. Grease a 900g/2lb loaf tin.
Line base with baking paper.

2. Beat butter, sugar in bowl with wooden spoon for 2–3 minutes
till light and creamy. Dribble eggs in gradually while beating. If mix
starts curdling, beat some flour in.

3. Sift flour over mix. Grate rind. Fold in with large metal spoon
using light movements (pg 10). Fold in milk, lemon juice.

4. Spoon into tin. Bake 55 minutes or till skewer comes out clean.

5. Mix sugar and juice for glaze. Prick cake all over with a skewer.
Pour glaze over. Take out of tin after 15 minutes. Cool on rack.

Iced Lemon Flatcake

Lemons and almonds make for luscious taste and texture.
This cake doesn't need to rise and is gluten-free.

1. Preheat oven to 150°C/300°F/gas 2. Prep a 20cm/8in square tin.
2. Cream butter and sugar until light, white, fluffy (pg 10).
3. Beat in a third of the egg, a third of the almonds. Repeat twice
till all in. Add lemon rind and juice/extract. Spoon into tin evenly.
4. Bake 30–40 minutes. Test. A cocktail stick should come out just
a bit sticky.
5. Cool in the tin. Remove. Make icing: mix sugar with juice for a
thick coating mix. Tip over cake. Add optional nuts, cherries.

MAKES
1

175g/6oz soft butter
175g/6oz caster sugar
3 large eggs, beaten
175g/6oz ground almonds
Grated rind of 2 lemons, no pith
A few drops of lemon juice or
    natural almond/vanilla extract

Icing
75g/3oz icing sugar, sifted
Juice of ½–1 lemon

MAKES 1

75g/3oz butter
110g/4oz caster sugar
1 large egg, beaten
Grated rind of 1 lemon/orange
225g/8oz self-raising flour
1 tsp baking powder
3 large ripe bananas
50g/2oz dates, snipped
½ tsp vanilla extract

Banana Tea Loaf

Loaf cakes don't have the drama of some but are easy to make and great for everyday. This classic's packed with energy and a great way to use up old bananas.

1. Preheat oven to 180°C/350°F/gas 4. Grease a 900g/2lb loaf tin. Line base.

2. Cream butter and sugar with a wooden spoon until very light and fluffy.

3. Beat in the egg vigorously, adding a pinch or two of flour if the mixture splits.

4. Add rind. Sift in flour, baking powder. Mix in lightly with a metal spoon.

5. Mash two bananas. Slice the other finely. Fold into mix with the dates. Add a splash of milk if mix is dry. Add vanilla extract.

6. Tip into tin. Bake 45–50 minutes. Test till a cocktail stick/skewer comes out clean. Leave in tin 5 minutes. Cool on rack. Eat as is or buttered.

YOU CAN

✱ sub in wholemeal flour for all or part quantity

✱ use oil instead of egg for vegans

✱ add walnuts, chopped hazelnuts, choc chips, cherries

✱ add some diced apple, plum or grated carrot

✱ brush with melted honey/water when hot or ice when cold

Carrot Cake

We always make this for my veggie sisters' birthdays.

MAKES 1

1. Preheat oven to 180°C/350°F/gas 4. Grease and line base and sides of 20cm/8in circular tin.

2. Tip sugar, honey, oil into bowl. Beat well with wooden spoon/balloon whisk. Add eggs, one at a time, beating between additions.

3. Sift in flour. Add cinnamon, salt, lemon rind and juice, carrots, nuts. Fold lightly together. Tip mix into tin.

4. Bake for 1 hour (skewer should come out clean). Cool in tin for 15 minutes. Turn out onto rack. Cool.

5. Make topping: beat cream cheese to soften. Add icing sugar and lemon juice gradually. Spread over cooled cake. Or make lemon icing (pg 87).

YOU CAN

* use lime/orange juice instead of lemon in the topping
* use grated peeled courgettes instead of carrots

175g/6oz caster sugar
2 tbsps honey
250ml/8fl oz sunflower oil
3 large eggs
175g/6oz self-raising wholemeal flour
1 tsp ground cinnamon
½ tsp salt
Grated rind of ½–1 lemon
Squeeze lemon juice
300g/10oz carrot, grated
150g/4–5oz pecans/walnuts, chopped

Topping
175g/6oz cream cheese
110–175g/4–6oz icing sugar, sifted
Juice of ½–1 lemon

MAKES
6

1 x 7g/¼oz sachet dried fast-action
   yeast
300ml/10fl oz lukewarm milk
450g/1lb strong white bread flour
1 tsp fine salt
2 pinches mixed spice
25g/1oz butter
25g/1oz caster sugar
50g/2oz currants
Extra milk for brushing

Yorkshire Teacakes

Well tasty and easy to make – knock these up from basic storecupboard ingredients.

1. Stir yeast into warm milk. Cover and leave to froth for 5–10 minutes.

2. Sift flour, salt, spice into a bowl. Rub butter in (pg 10).

3. Add sugar, currants. Add frothy milk to the mix with a fork or your fingers. Draw dough into a soft ball.

4. Knead on a floured board for 8 minutes (pg 11).

5. Sit dough in a bowl. Cover and leave till doubled in size (1–2 hours, depending on temperature).

6. Knead dough for 1 minute. Divide into six. Roll out into 15cm/6in rounds. Sit on greased trays till doubled.

7. Heat oven to 200°C/400°F/gas 6. Brush buns with milk. Bake 20 minutes or till cooked and golden.

YOU CAN

✱ top each bun with icing (pg 77) and a cherry.

✱ make Fruit Loaf. Add more spice and chopped cherries to dough at step 3. At step 6 put dough into a 450g/1lb loaf tin to rise. Bake for 30 minutes.

Apple Cake

Moist and fruity, this big cake never disappoints. Enjoy for tea (or breakfast) or warm as a pudding with crème fraîche, yogurt or ice-cream.

675g/1½lb cooking apples
75g/3oz softened butter
175g/6oz soft brown sugar
2 large eggs, beaten
225g/8oz plain flour
2 tsps baking powder
½ tsp ground mixed spice
½ tsp ground cinnamon
1 tbsp marmalade/apricot jam
Grated rind of 1 lemon
1–2 tbsps milk
3 drops almond extract (optional)
Dusting of icing sugar

1. Preheat oven to 180°C/350°F/gas 4. Grease and line a 20cm/8in round deep, loose-based cake tin.

2. Peel, core and chop apples into 5mm/¼in chunks.

3. Cream butter, sugar (pg 10). Beat eggs in gradually.

4. Sift flour, baking powder, spices and fold in lightly (pg 10).

5. Add apple, marmalade/jam, lemon rind. Gradually add milk (and almond extract if using) till the mix is soft enough to drop off the spoon. Spoon into tin.

6. Bake 1 hour – a skewer or cocktail stick should come out clean.

7. Remove. Cool on rack. Turn out. Top with sifted icing sugar.

YOU CAN

* mix pears and plums in with apples
* add dates or dates and walnuts to the mix
* top with lemon butter icing

50g/2oz dark chocolate
1 tsp vanilla extract
175g/6oz plain flour
2 tbsps cocoa
1 tsp baking powder
½ tsp bicarbonate of soda
150g/5oz soft brown sugar
2 tbsps golden syrup
150ml/5fl oz sunflower/vegetable oil
75ml/3fl oz sour cream
2 large eggs

Fudge icing
275g/10oz icing sugar, sifted
25g/1oz cocoa powder, sifted
110g/4oz butter, melted
3–4 tbsps water

Chocolate Fudge Birthday Cake

Rich, dark and beautiful, this makes the perfect birthday cake. Decorate tastefully… or disgracefully.

1. Melt chocolate in bowl over pan of water (pg 12). Add vanilla extract. Set aside.

2. Preheat oven to 170°C/325°F/gas 3. Grease and line two 18cm/7½in cake tins. Grease lining. Sift flour, cocoa, baking powder, bicarb into a bowl.

3. Add rest of ingredients. Beat hard 2–3 minutes until creamy.

4. Divide between tins. Bake 30 minutes (check after 20) till sponge starts to shrink from sides, a cocktail sticks comes out clean. Invert and cool on a rack. Then, make icing.

5. Mix sugar and cocoa together. Beat in mixed butter and water till thick and smooth. Spread half on one cake. Sandwich. Add more icing, candles, sweets, fresh cherries, berries or pipe a message.

Victoria Sponge Cake

Quintessentially English – make this the centrepiece of an afternoon tea event or turn the mix into wicked fairy cakes.

1. Preheat oven to 180°C/350°F/gas 4. Grease two 18cm/7½in cake tins. Line bases. Beat everything with an electric whisk.
2. Or by hand: cream butter and sugar till light and fluffy (pg 10). Beat eggs in, one at a time, with 1 tbsp flour.
3. Sift remaining flour and baking powder over bowl. Add vanilla extract. Fold in gently (pg 10). Divide evenly between tins.
4. Bake for 25 minutes or till risen, firm, shrinking from edges. Leave in tins for 3 minutes. Invert onto rack. Remove paper. Cool on racks. Fill with jam and cream. Sprinkle icing sugar.

YOU CAN
✷ make iced Fairy Cakes. Spoon a little mix into each of 12–14 bun cases sitting in tins. Add a little jam. Top with more mix. Bake 20 minutes. Cool. Icing: beat together 325g/12oz icing sugar, 150g/5oz cream cheese, 75g/3oz soft butter, vanilla extract.

MAKES 1

175g/6oz soft butter
175g/6oz sugar
3 eggs
175g/6oz self-raising flour, sifted
1 tsp baking powder
1 tsp vanilla extract

To fill
Jam
Whipped cream

To top
Icing sugar, sifted

225g/8oz self-raising flour
1 tsp baking powder
Pinch salt
50g/2oz butter, cubed
25g/1oz caster sugar
150ml/5fl oz milk
Beaten egg to brush (optional)
Granulated sugar to top

Sweet Scones

Want light scones? Handle dough lightly.

1. Preheat oven to 220°C/425°F/gas 7. Grease a baking tray.

2. Sift flour, baking powder, salt into a bowl.

3. Add bits of butter. Amalgamate by rubbing into flour, using your fingertips. Keep it light.

4. Add sugar. Add milk gradually, mixing in with a fork.

5. Gather dough into a ball. Place on a floured surface. Roll out very gently until 2.5cm/1in thick. Cut into 5cm/2in rounds with a cutter/glass, or into triangles. Repeat.

6. Sit well apart on a baking tray. Brush with egg. Sprinkle sugar.

7. Bake for 12–15 minutes till risen, golden. Cool on a rack. Eat with butter, jam, whipped cream. Enjoy with a cuppa.

YOU CAN
* add chopped dates, grated lemon or orange rind, sultanas
* make Cheese Scones. At step 2 increase quantity of baking powder to 4 tsps. At step 3, omit sugar, add a bit of mustard, cayenne, chilli powder, 50g/2oz grated Cheddar. Bake 10–12 minutes.

Cheese Fat Rascals

Think cheese straw meets scone – designed for those who don't have a sweet tooth but want to join in with something delicious. A substantial tea item and perfect for picnics.

1. Preheat oven to 200°C/400°F/gas 6. Grease a baking tray.
2. Mix dry ingredients in a bowl – saving half the olives and tomatoes, a bit of cheese for topping. Beat in milk and mustard.
3. Place dough on a lightly floured surface. Knead gently for 1 minute.
4. Roll out lightly. Cut into 6 triangles or circles. Brush tops with a little oil. Scatter olives, tomatoes, cheese. Bake 20 minutes or till cooked through. Cool. Split and eat warm or cold with butter/ cream cheese. Good with celery, chutney in a veggie Ploughman's.

YOU CAN
* sub spring onion with 1 onion, finely chopped and fried in butter

MAKES 6

225g/8oz plain bread flour
225g/8oz wholemeal bread flour
½–1 tsp salt
2 pinches chilli or cayenne powder
2 tsps bicarbonate of soda
2 tsps cream of tartar
225g/8oz strong Cheddar, grated
6–8 spring onions, chopped
A few black olives, chopped and whole
A few sundried tomatoes, chopped
300ml/½ pint milk
1 tsp strong mustard

Drop Scones

Everyone loves these and they're pretty foolproof. Enjoy with lemon curd, honey or jam and butter.

1. Sift flour, salt, sugar into a bowl. Add eggs and a bit of milk. Beat well.
2. Whisk in remaining milk, bit by bit, till smooth. Put a frying pan on to medium heat. Brush with melted butter.
3. Drop single tablespoonfuls of batter onto pan, well apart. Cook 1–2 minutes till browned on the base, bubbling on top. Flip and repeat. Keep warm in a tea towel.

MAKES 12   **EXPRESS**

225g/8oz self-raising flour
Pinch salt
1 tbsp caster sugar
2 eggs
300ml/½ pint milk
25–50g/1–2oz butter, melted, for frying

Classic White Loaf

Perfect for everything from sandwiches to toast, this tastes amazing – and you know what's in it. Keep bread flour and yeast in.

1. Sift flour, salt into a bowl. Add butter and rub in (pg 10).
2. Add yeast and sugar. Add water. Mix with your hands or a wooden spoon. Pull into a soft warm dough.
3. Knead on a floured surface for 8–10 minutes (pg 11) till elastic.
4. Sit in a bowl. Cover. Leave 1–2 hours or till doubled in size.
5. Knead 2 minutes. Shape to fit tin. Cover and leave till it rises over the top of the tin. Brush with milk or beaten egg and milk.
6. Bake in a preheated oven at 230°C/450°F/gas 8 for 30 minutes. Turn out. Tap the base – it should sound hollow. If not, cook another 5–10 minutes. Cool on a rack.

YOU CAN

✱ shape dough into rolls at step 5. Sit to rise and bake on tray for 10–15 minutes. Cook as above for 15 minutes or till done.

MAKES 1

VEGAN OPT.

700g/1½lb white bread flour
2 tsps salt
15g/½oz butter/margarine
1 x 7g/¼oz sachet dried fast-action yeast
½ tsp sugar
425ml/15fl oz warm water
Milk or beaten egg for brushing

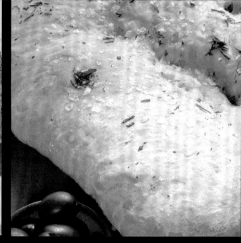

Mum's Treacle Bread

2 heaped tbsps black treacle
Approx 850ml/1½ pints warm
**   water**
2 x 7g/¼oz sachet dried fast-
**   action yeast**
450g/1lb wholemeal bread flour
450g/1lb white bread flour
1 tsp salt

1. Grease inside and rims of
two 900g/2lb loaf tins.
2. Mix treacle with 150ml/5oz warm
water. Add yeast. Stir. Cover. Leave
5–10 minutes till frothy.
3. Meantime, sift flours, salt into large
bowl.
4. Add yeast mix to remaining
700ml/1¼ pints warm water.
5. Stir into flours for a very loose
sticky dough.
6. Spoon into tins. Cover. Leave to
rise 15 minutes or just higher than
the tin (not spilling over).
7. Preheat oven to 200°C/400°F/gas 6.
Bake 30–40 minutes till cooked. Turn
out. It's done when base sounds
hollow when tapped.

YOU CAN

✱ use all white or all brown flour
✱ use honey instead of treacle
✱ add a handful oats/muesli

Irish Soda Bread

225g/8oz plain white flour
225g/8oz wholemeal flour
1 tsp salt
1 good tsp bicarbonate of soda
450ml buttermilk/sour milk/milk
**   soured with lemon juice**

1. Preheat oven to 200°C/400°F/gas 6.
2. Mix flours, salt, bicarb in a bowl.
3. Pour milk into a well in the centre.
4. Beat with a wooden spoon or mix
with a stretched hand, stirring from
the well to the edges. Pull into a ball.
5. Sit dough on a lightly floured
board. Pat into a loaf about 5cm/2in
thick.
6. Sprinkle extra flour on a baking
tray. Sit bread on it. Cut a deep cross
into the top. Bake 25–30 minutes. Tap
base. It should sound hollow. Return
till it does.

Italian Flatbread

350g/12oz white bread flour
½ tsp fine salt
1 x 7g/¼oz sachet dried fast-
**   action yeast**
5 tbsps olive oil
200–250g/7–8fl oz warm water
Sprigs fresh rosemary, chopped
Black olives
Sundried tomato (optional)
Crushed sea salt

1. Mix sifted flour, fine salt, yeast.
Add 3 tbsps olive oil, water, rosemary.
2. Mix with your hands. Pull together
for a soft, warm dough. Knead on
lightly floured surface, 8–10 minutes.
3. Sit dough in a bowl. Cover. Leave to
double in size – 1 hour plus.
4. Brush a 30cm/12in pizza tray with
oil. Knead risen dough for 2 minutes.
5. Roll and stretch dough to fit tin.
Poke all over to indent. Cover. Leave
to rise for 20–30 minutes.
6. Stick olives, sprigs of rosemary into
dough. Scatter sea salt.
8. Drizzle remaining oil. Bake at
220°C/425°F/gas 7 for 20 minutes.

DINNER

PIZZA

Homestyle pizzas are fun to make, cheaper, tastier and much healthier.

450g/1lb strong white bread flour
1 tsp salt
1 tsp caster sugar
2 x 7g/¼oz sachets fast-action dried
  yeast
300ml/½pint warm water
2 tbsps olive oil

All-Purpose Pizza Dough

Bang any topping on this olive-oil pizza base.

1. Tip sifted flour, salt, sugar, yeast into a bowl. Add water, oil.
2. Mixing with your hands, pull into a soft, smooth dough ball.
3. Knead on lightly floured board for 10 minutes (pg 11) till elastic.
4. Leave in a bowl in a warm place, covered with film or a damp tea towel, until doubled in size (1 hour plus). Knead for 2 minutes.
5. Divide and roll into 2 large/4 small pizzas. Leave to rise on tins for 10 minutes. Top and cook as per recipe, or freeze bases.

1 x basic dough (above)
1–2 tbsps tomato sauce (pg 106) or
  passata mixed with 1 clove garlic,
  crushed, seasoning
A few black olives
A few basil leaves
Olive oil

No-Rise Speedy Pizza

As your main dough's rising, make a cheat's griddled pizza.

1. Make all-purpose dough up to end of step 3. Break a bit off and leave rest of dough to rise.
2. Preheat grill and a griddle or frying pan. Brush pan with oil.
3. Roll your portion of dough into a thin pizza. Griddle or fry for 1 minute or till just browning. Turn and repeat. Remove.
4. Spread thinly with tomato sauce/passata. Scatter toppings. Drizzle oil. Grill 1–2 minutes or till slightly charring, hot and crispy.

1 x basic dough (above)
1–2 sprigs rosemary, chopped
2 cloves garlic, sliced
Tub pitted olives
1 ball/bar mozzarella
Milk for brushing

Dough Balls

For sharing around and for starters.

1. Knead rosemary and garlic into all-purpose dough at step 3. Break bits off. **Plain**: roll into neat walnut-sized balls. **Stuffed**: make small circles. Place olive/bit of cheese on each. Pull dough up and over. Pinch to seal firmly. Sit seam-down on baking tray.
2. Brush with milk. Bake 15 minutes at 220°C/425°F/gas 7. Serve dipped into soft garlic butter/warmed tomato sauce (pg 106).

House Pizza

Heat up a big slice of this when you're just in after a hard day or a big night out. Make loads for parties.

1. Make dough to end of step 3. Roll to fit 1–2 large greased trays.

2. Leave on tea-towel-covered trays till doubled – maybe 1 hour.

3. Meantime, make toppings. **Margherita**: make tomato sauce or mix passata with crushed garlic and seasoning.

4. Onion & olive: fry onions, garlic very gently in oil for 20 minutes or till soft and pale gold. Preheat oven to 220°C/425°F/ gas 7.

5. Top them: spread tomato topping over one pizza – scatter remaining ingredients.

6. Spread onion topping over the second. Sprinkle herbs, seasoning and arrange olives in a pattern.

7. Drizzle oil. Season. Cook 20 minutes or till base is crispy.

YOU CAN
* put two toppings onto one pizza
* add goat's cheese or garlic mushrooms to the onion topping
* griddle thinly sliced aubergine – add to tomato topping
* use thinly rolled puff pastry, or top your frozen bases

FEEDS 6 VEGAN OPT.

1 or 2 x basic dough (pg 100)

Margherita topping

1 x tomato sauce (pg 106) or passata mixed with 1 clove garlic, crushed
Dried oregano/fresh basil
12 black olives
Freshly grated Parmesan/Cheddar
Sliced mozzarella
Olive oil

Onion & olive topping

700g/1½lb onions, peeled and thinly sliced
2–3 cloves garlic, crushed
2 tbsps olive oil
12 black olives
Dried thyme/oregano/sage or fresh basil
Salt and pepper
Olive oil

Pizza Florentine

Tastes as good as it looks – a useful pre-exam brain boost.

1 x frozen or fresh pizza base
Handful young spinach
A little olive oil
Squeeze lemon juice
1 clove garlic, sliced
Salt and pepper
3–4 tbsps tomato sauce (pg 106) or
   passata mixed with 1 clove garlic,
   crushed, seasoning
Sprinkling of Parmesan/Cheddar
1 egg

1. Make dough (pg 100) to end of step 5. Roll out to fit a greased pizza tray. Cover with a tea towel. Leave to rise for 15 minutes.
2. Preheat oven 220°C/425°F/gas 7.
3. Meantime, slam spinach into pan with a splash of water. Heat to wilt. Drain. Squeeze out excess moisture. Drizzle with oil, lemon. Add garlic. Season.
4. Spread tomato sauce over fresh or frozen base. Add spinach, cheese. Drizzle a little oil. Cook 8 minutes. Crack egg onto middle. Cook 8 minutes or till egg sets.

YOU CAN try these toppings…

✱ roasted veg: spread tomato sauce, garlic, roast or griddled mediterranean veg, cheese
✱ marinara: blend 2 big tomatoes, basil, seasoning or use passata with added crushed garlic. Spread over base with sliced garlic, oregano.
✱ funghi: top with fried onion, mushrooms fried with garlic, goat's cheese, thyme/basil
✱ garlic bread: spread garlic butter and herbs or puréed tomato sauce with garlic
✱ crudo: spread mix of raw chopped tomatoes, basil, oil, olives
✱ calzone: roll the dough into circles as for pasties (pg 146). Fill with tomato sauce, mozzarella, ricotta, spinach. Fold over, seal and bake.

Chip-Butty Pizza

Awesomely simple and cheap and it tastes gorgeous.

1. Make dough to end of step 5 (pg 100). Roll out. Rise on greased trays under tea towel for 15 minutes.

2. Preheat oven to 220°C/425°F/gas 7. Meantime, boil potatoes for 4–5 minutes. Don't let them break up. Drain well.

3. Gently fry onion in oil till soft, not coloured. Top freshly risen or frozen bases with a layer of onion then potato.

4. Brush lightly with oil. Scatter rosemary, salt and pepper. Bake 10–15 minutes till base is crisp, potatoes browned and tender.

YOU CAN
* add grated Cheddar/Gruyère, blobs low-fat crème fraîche
* make White Pizza – brush fresh/frozen bases with oil. Rub with cut garlic. Layer thinly sliced mozzarella. Season. Bake. Serve with chopped tomatoes, basil, olives alongside.

FEEDS 2   **VEGAN**

2 frozen bases or 1 x pizza dough
2 large unpeeled old potatoes
   or 6–8 large salad potatoes, in
   5mm/¼ in slices
1 medium onion, thinly sliced
3–4 tbsps olive oil
2 sprigs fresh rosemary, finely
   chopped
Sea salt
Black pepper

PASTA

Pasta's a brilliant base for extraordinary sauces. Cook it properly (pg 12) so it doesn't glue up. Team with salads and good bread.

Spaghetti/Linguine with Garlic & Chilli

Feeds 1
110g/4oz spaghetti/linguine
1½ tbsps olive oil
2 fat cloves garlic, sliced
½–1 de-seeded, finely chopped chilli or a few chilli flakes
Parsley, finely chopped, or basil (optional)
Squeeze lemon juice
Salt and pepper

1. Add pasta to boiling salted water. Set timer as per pack instructions.
2. Heat oil gently in pan. Add garlic. Stir to soften without colouring.
3. Add chilli, herb, lemon, salt, pepper. Stir into drained pasta.

YOU CAN

✳ add a few drained chickpeas, pinenuts, olives
✳ make sauce with ½ tsp cracked black pepper, 50g/2oz cheese, pasta water
✳ slice mushrooms. Fry in oil/butter/crushed garlic. Add cream/crème fraîche, thyme/tarragon. Season. Mix into pasta.
✳ mix pasta water, butter/cream, crumbled blue cheese
✳ make Pasta Caprese. Add raw chopped cherry tomatoes, mozzarella, rocket, oil, garlic to hot pasta.

Conchiglie & Pesto

Feeds 1
110g/4oz shell pasta
Parmesan, grated
Pinenuts
Black pepper

Pesto
110g/4oz fresh basil
150ml/5fl oz olive oil
25g/1oz pinenuts
2 cloves garlic
½ tsp salt
150ml/5fl oz olive oil

50g/2oz grated Parmesan

1. Add pasta to boiling salted water. Set timer as per pack instructions.
2. Make pesto (pg 187). Drain pasta.
3. Stir in 1–2 tbsps pesto. Add more Parmesan, pinenuts, pepper.

YOU CAN

✳ mix sundried tomato purée with crushed garlic and oil – stir into hot shells
✳ buy good pesto
✳ grow your own basil

Tagliatelle & Chilli Fried Egg

Feeds 1

   110g/4oz tagliatelle
   1 tbsp olive oil
   1 tsp butter
   1 clove garlic, thinly sliced
   1–2 large eggs
   Dried chilli flakes
   Parmesan/other cheese
   Salt and pepper
   Basil

1. Cook pasta. Four minutes before done, heat oil, butter in frying pan.
2. Add garlic. Stir 1 minute without colouring. Add eggs. Fry till done.
3. Drain pasta. Tip back into its pan. Add a little chilli, cheese, seasoning.
4. Tip pasta onto warm plate. Top with eggs, oily juices, chilli flakes, basil.

YOU CAN

* top egg with chilli jam
* top/toss pasta in tomato sauce (pg 106). Top with egg.

* toss pasta in pesto (pg 187) or sundried tomato paste

Sausage & Mustard Cream

Feeds 1

   110g/4oz penne
   2–3 veggie sausages
   A little oil for frying
   A little butter
   2–3 tbsps cream
   Salt and pepper
   1 tsp mustard
   Grated cheese to taste
   Fresh herbs – parsley/basil/ sage/thyme

1. Put pasta on to cook in boiling salted water.
2. Fry sausages in a little oil, or grill as pack directs.
3. Drain pasta. Melt butter in warm pasta pan. Add cream, seasoning, mustard to heat through. Add pasta, cheese, herb, sliced sausage.

4. Taste and adjust seasoning. Top with more cheese. Eat with salad.

YOU CAN

* brush sausages with ketchup, honey
* griddle or fry diagonal slices of courgette. Sub for sausages.

Roasted Cherry Tomato Pasta

Feeds 1

   110g linguine/spaghetti/ tagliatelle
   Handful cherry tomatoes
   Olive oil
   1 clove garlic, sliced
   Thyme/oregano
   Salt and pepper

Garlic breadcrumbs

   1–2 slices crustless stale/fresh bread
   Knob butter
   1 clove garlic, crushed
   Lemon rind (optional)

1. Put pasta on to cook. Preheat oven to 200°C/400°F/gas 6.
2. Toss tomatoes in oil, garlic, thyme in roasting tin/dish. Season. Roast till skins are just splitting.
3. Meantime, make garlic breadcrumbs. Tear bread and blitz with handblender. Fry gently in butter, garlic till crisp, browned. Stir in a little lemon rind if desired.
4. Drain pasta. Slap back into pan with tomatoes, oily juices. Serve topped with breadcrumbs.

YOU CAN

* add grated cheese
* roast the tomatoes with fresh basil, rosemary, oregano

Muddled Tomato Spaghetti

Feeds 2

225g/8oz spaghetti
350g/12oz cherry tomatoes
2 tbsps olive oil
1 clove garlic, sliced
Handful black olives, chopped
1–2 tsps capers, drained
Pinch chilli flakes
Pinch sugar
Baby spinach
Salt and pepper
Fresh basil, torn
Parmesan, grated

1. Put pasta on to cook in boiling salted water as pack directs.
2. Cut tomatoes in half. Remove seeds with a teaspoon.
3. Warm olive oil in a pan. Add garlic to soften, not colour.
4. Add tomatoes, olives, capers, chilli, sugar, spinach, bit of basil. Season.
5. Boil, reduce heat immediately. Simmer a few minutes.
6. Add hot drained pasta to sauce. Season. Tip into bowls/plates.
7. Top with torn basil, grated cheese, garlic breadcrumbs (pg 103).

YOU CAN

✱ make Puttanesca sauce. Gently fry 3 cloves crushed garlic, 1 de-seeded chilli till soft, not coloured. Add 440g/14oz tin chopped tomatoes. Add pinch sugar, 175g/6oz black olives, 1 tbsp capers, salt and pepper. Simmer for 20 minutes. Stir into pasta with a little oil and fresh basil.

Chic Lemon Pasta

Feeds 1–2

175g/6oz tagliatelle/linguine/ spaghetti
Rind and juice of 1 lemon
1–2 tbsps crème fraîche
Salt and pepper
A few baby spinach/rocket leaves
Parmesan/other cheese, grated

1. Put pasta on to cook. Grate lemon rind into a bowl with crème fraîche, seasoning.
2. Drain pasta. Tip back into warm pan with spinach. Stir to wilt spinach. Add cheese.
3. Stir lemon juice into crème fraîche. Mix into pasta. Top with cheese.

YOU CAN

✱ whisk 2 tbsps lemon juice, 6 tbsps olive oil. Add 2 tbsps cheese. Whisk. Season. Tip into hot pasta with basil, 2 tbsps pasta water.

Lifesaver Tomato Pasta Sauce

Feeds 3–4

Olive oil
1 medium onion, very finely chopped
2 cloves garlic, crushed
Pinch salt
2 x 400g/14oz cans chopped tomatoes
Pinch sugar
Black pepper
Squeeze lemon
Fresh or dried basil/thyme/ oregano
1–2 tbsps tomato purée
350g/12oz penne/spaghetti
Butter/extra oil
Parmesan/Cheddar, freshly grated

1. Heat oil gently in a pan. Add onion, garlic, salt. Cook to soften over low heat for 5–10 minutes without colouring.

2. Add tomatoes, sugar. Simmer very gently for 15–20 minutes. Stir occasionally. Season, taste, adjust the balance of flavour with lemon, herbs, purée. Cool for later or use now.

3. Meantime, cook pasta. Drain. Slap back into pan. Add a bit of butter, oil. To serve: stir sauce into pasta or pile on top. Add grated cheese or garlic breadcrumbs (pg 103).

4. Or put pasta and sauce into heatproof bowls, top with cheese and/or breadcrumbs. Grill till bubbling.

YOU CAN

* blitz sauce with handblender for a smooth result

* run a little pesto into finished sauce on plate
* stir in a splash of balsamic vinegar
* add 2 tbsps cream/mascarpone/ Philadelphia cheese at end of step 2
* add whole red chilli, dried chilli or flakes for heat
* add 1–2 chopped, de-seeded red/ orange peppers at step 1
* dice a bit of mozzarella into hot sauce just before serving
* soften 2 bashed cloves garlic in olive oil. Simmer with 1 can chopped tomatoes, oregano, sugar, salt, pepper, Tabasco for 10 minutes.

* bake it. Layer up tomato sauce, cooked or left-over pasta, grated cheese, fried sliced aubergine. Top with cheese or sauce (pg 158). Cook 30 minutes at 200°C/400°F/gas 6.

Mushroom & Asparagus Carbonara

Feeds 2

    225g/8oz penne
    200g/7oz asparagus, tough end
        cut away
    Garlic breadcrumbs (pg 105)
    2 large field or a few chestnut/
        white mushrooms
    Knob of butter
    2 large eggs
    Parmesan/other cheese
    Salt and pepper
    Bit of parsley (optional)

1. Put pasta on to cook. Boil asparagus in frying pan for 2 minutes or till tender/crisp. Drain. Cut into diagonals. Make garlic breadcrumbs.

2. Fry mushrooms lightly in butter. Set aside. Beat eggs with 1 tbsp cheese, seasoning.

3. Drain pasta. Return to warm pan with butter. Tip eggs in. Turn briefly to coat the pasta without scrambling the eggs. Add veg. Tip onto plates. Top with crispy crumbs, optional parsley and/or grated cheese.

YOU CAN

* add peas/broad beans instead of mushrooms
* use sliced/ribboned courgette instead of asparagus
* add 1–2 tbsps cream/crème fraîche

Tagliatelle with Mixed Mushrooms

Feeds 2

    4 nests tagliatelle
    2 cloves garlic, diced
    1–2 tbsps olive oil
    110g/4oz exotic mushrooms, sliced
    110g/4oz mixed white/chestnut mushrooms, sliced
    Thyme
    Lemon juice
    Salt and pepper
    Grated cheese/garlic breadcrumbs (pg 105)

1. Cook pasta as pack directs.

2. 5 minutes before it's ready, add garlic to oil in heated pan.

3. Add all the mushrooms after a few seconds. Turn to coat.

4. Cook for 3–4 minutes. Add thyme, lemon, seasoning.

5. Drain pasta. Add contents of the pan. Serve with cheese/breadcrumbs.

YOU CAN

✳ add crumbled chilli/a bit of cream

✳ top with rocket, watercress

All-in-One Veg Pasta

Feeds 1

    4–5 small salad potatoes
    Garlic breadcrumbs (pg 105)
    1–2 nests tagliatelle
    Handful fresh thin green beans, ends trimmed
    Salt and pepper
    Bit of pesto (homemade (pg 104) or bought) or butter/oil

1. Put potatoes to boil in a large pan of lightly salted water.

2. Meantime, make garlic breadcrumbs.

3. Judge when potatoes are just getting tender and add pasta to the pan. 3 minutes before pasta's ready, add the beans. Cook till tender.

4. Drain veg and pasta. Tip back into warm pan. Season. Add a little pesto or butter/oil. Serve with scattered garlic breadcrumbs.

YOU CAN

✳ add peas, broccoli, chickpeas

Aubergine & Tomato Pasta

Feeds 3–4

    Olive oil
    1 onion, finely chopped
    2 cloves garlic, crushed
    A few chilli flakes

2 x 400g/14oz cans chopped
tomatoes
1 tsp sugar
Salt and black pepper
400g/14oz tagliatelle/penne
1 large aubergine, trimmed,
diced
A few black olives (optional)
Fresh basil
Parmesan/Cheddar, grated

1. Heat 2 tbsps oil in a pan. Cook
onion gently till soft, not coloured.
2. Add garlic, chilli. Cook further 2
minutes. Add tomatoes, sugar, salt,
pepper.
3. Boil. Reduce heat. Simmer gently
for 10–20 minutes till thick and saucy.
4. Meantime, put pasta on to cook.
5. To cook aubergine, heat 2 tbsps oil
in a frying pan. Fry for a few minutes
till tender. Add to tomato sauce.
6. Drain pasta. Toss with sauce and
optional olives. Add basil. Serve with
cheese.

Orecchiette & Crunchy Broccoli

Feeds 2
175g/6oz orecchiette
Garlic breadcrumbs (pg 105)
175g/6oz broccoli florets
1–2 tbsps olive oil or oil/butter
Salt and pepper
Freshly grated Parmesan/
Cheddar (optional)

1. Put pasta on. Prep and cook garlic
breadcrumbs (pg 105).
2. Boil separate pan of water. Add
broccoli 4–5 minutes before pasta's
ready. Boil 4–5 minutes or till just
tender. Drain.

3. Drain pasta. Tip back into warm
pan. Add broccoli, oil/butter, seasoning,
a quarter of the crisp crumbs. Stir.
4. Tip into bowls. Top with remaining
crumbs, optional cheese.

YOU CAN
* use penne or any pasta shape
* boil water in a kettle first. Pour into
pan to save time/energy/cash.

Roast Veg & Tagliatelle

Feeds 1
Handful baby/other waxy new
potatoes
4 shallots/small onions,
quartered, skins on
Handful cherry tomatoes
Drizzle of balsamic/white wine
vinegar
1 tsp sugar
Salt and pepper
75g/3oz tagliatelle

Oil mix
A few basil leaves
Salt
2 tsps pesto
Thyme
3–4 tbsps olive oil

1. Boil potatoes 5–10 minutes till
almost tender. Drain well. Preheat
oven to 220°C/400°F/gas 6.
2. Make oil mix: bash basil with
salt using pestle and mortar (or
bowl). Add pesto, thyme, oil.
3. Crush potatoes a bit with a fork.
Place in roasting tin/dish with shallots/
onions, cherry tomatoes.
4. Drizzle with oil mix and mixed
vinegar/sugar. Season. Roast
20–30 minutes till potatoes are
unctuous, crisping, tomato squashy.
5. Meantime, cook and drain pasta.
Season. Top with roasted veg and all
the tasty oily scrapings.

YOU CAN
* scatter garlic breadcrumbs (pg 105)
* roast chunks of lemon in the dish
* use old or sweet potato or
butternut squash
* add unpeeled garlic cloves to
roasting tin 5 minutes before serving

FEEDS 2–3

225g/8oz macaroni
50g/2oz butter
50g/2oz plain white flour
600ml/1 pint milk
200g/7oz strong Cheddar, grated
1 tsp English mustard
1 tbsp lemon juice
Salt and pepper
Extra cheese for topping

Macaroni Cheese

Great comfort food. Make sure you use a good strong Cheddar to give the sauce character.

1. Boil pasta hard for 15 minutes. Drain. Preheat oven to 200°C/400°F/gas 6. Meantime, make sauce.

2. Melt butter gently in a pan. Add flour. Cook gently, stirring paste, for 2 minutes. Remove. Beat milk in very gradually with a wooden spoon/balloon whisk for a smooth sauce. Return to low heat. Stir until it boils and thickens.

3. Simmer gently 5–10 minutes. Add cheese, mustard, juice, seasoning (extra milk if too thick). Add pasta. Bake in a buttered dish/tin 20–30 mins till browned, bubbling, or grill it.

YOU CAN
✱ top with 2 tbsps fresh breadcrumbs or garlic butter or sliced tomatoes
✱ add cooked, drained spinach or line base with tomato sauce
✱ make Leek Cheese. Boil white bit of leeks till tender. Drain. Place in buttered shallow dish. Top with sauce. Bake or grill.

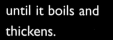

Gnocchi

Tasty Italian potato dumplings with two great sauces.

1. Boil potatoes till tender. Drain well. Return to pan, covered. Leave 5 minutes. Mash till absolutely smooth.

2. Use your hands to mix the mash with flour and salt on a board or in a bowl. Knead into a smooth ball.

3. Divide into 4. Roll into long sausages as thick as a thumb, cut into 2cm/¾in long bits. Mark lightly with a fork. Cover with a tea towel.

4. Bring a large pan of water to boil. Reduce to a simmer. Add a few gnocchi. Cook for 3 minutes.

5. Remove. Drain. Turn in olive oil if using later/next day.

6. Sauce 1: heat tomato sauce. **Sauce 2**: melt butter, stir in lemon juice, herbs, seasoning.

7. Serve gnocchi with one sauce or both. Sprinkle with cheese. Eat with salad.

YOU CAN

✱ drop into greased small dishes or one big dish. Add tomato sauce, cheese. Or dot with blue cheese/Gruyère & crème fraîche. Bake till hot and bubbling.

FEEDS 2–3   VEGAN

Gnocchi

450g/1lb floury old potatoes, peeled
225g/8oz plain white flour
Salt
Olive oil, if not using immediately

Sauce 1

1 x tomato sauce (pg 106)

Sauce 2

50g/2oz butter
Juice of 1 lemon
Fresh basil/sage/parsley
Salt and pepper

Parmesan/Cheddar for sprinkling

1 x tomato sauce (pg 106)
1 x cheese sauce (pg 110)

Filling

25g/1oz butter
1 small onion, finely chopped
1 clove garlic
2 x 160g/6oz packs spinach or same weight loose spinach
1 x 250g/9oz tub ricotta cheese, crumbled
100g/4oz feta cheese, crumbled
Small pinch nutmeg (optional)
Salt and pepper
A few leaves fresh basil, chopped
12 no-pre-cook cannelloni tubes
Parmesan/other hard cheese, grated

Cannelloni with Ricotta & Spinach

An impressive dinner dish – great for entertaining.

1. Make tomato sauce (pg 106) and cheese sauce (pg 110). Preheat oven to 200°C/400°F/gas 6. Grease a shallow baking dish.

2. Heat butter in a large pan. Cook onion, garlic gently on low heat for 5 minutes till soft, not coloured. Add spinach, stirring to soften and wilt. Cool 5 minutes.

3. Add ricotta, feta, nutmeg if using, seasoning, basil. Mix with a fork, keeping it textured. Stuff into the pasta using a teaspoon.

4. Layer dish with tomato sauce, stuffed tubes, grated cheese, tomato sauce, cheese sauce, grated cheese. Bake 30–40 minutes.

YOU CAN

* fill rolled pancakes or large cooked pasta shells – bake as above
* add grated lemon rind, other herbs to the filling
* use spinach stuffing to layer into lasagne with tomato sauce

Lasagne al Forno

There's nothing like lasagne to feed a load of people. This one's full of summery flavours but feel free to customize.

1. Make tomato sauce (pg 106) and cheese sauce (pg 110). Preheat oven to 200°C/400°F/gas 6. Grease a lasagne or large ovenproof dish, at least 5cm/2in deep.

2. Heat oil and butter in a large pan. Add garlic to soften on a very low heat without colouring.

3. Add courgette slices and herbs. Cook gently for a few minutes to tenderize.

4. Layer up the dish with tomato sauce, sheets of pasta, courgettes, grated cheese, a little cheese sauce, more tomato sauce and so on. Finish with pasta and a layer of cheese sauce. Bake 30 minutes or till golden. Rest it for 5 minutes before eating.

YOU CAN

✱ layer with roasted veg (pg 109), Ratatouille (pg 155), ricotta & spinach (pg 112)

✱ make in 4 individual dishes. Cook one, freeze 3.

✱ use layers of pancakes or sliced cooked potato instead of pasta

FEEDS 4–6　**VEGAN OPT.**

2 x tomato sauce (pg 106)
1 x cheese sauce (pg 110) plus extra cheese
1–2 tbsps oil and a little butter
1–2 flat cloves garlic, sliced
4–5 large courgettes, thinly sliced diagonally
½ tsp dried oregano or dill/fresh parsley, finely chopped (optional)
Salt and pepper
1 pack no-pre-cook lasagne

NOODLES

Veg and noodles make a great match. Pull them together with exciting sauces. Add nuts, eggs or tofu to boost nutrition.

FEEDS 2 · VEGAN · EXPRESS

150g/5oz dried egg noodles

Sauce

¾ tbsp soy sauce
½ tsp sesame oil
2½ tbsps hot water/stock
Pinch sugar

Stir-fry

½ tbsp grated/finely chopped ginger
3 cloves garlic, finely sliced
4 spring onions, finely sliced
110g/4 oz beansprouts
¾ tbsp groundnut/sunflower oil
Splash sesame oil

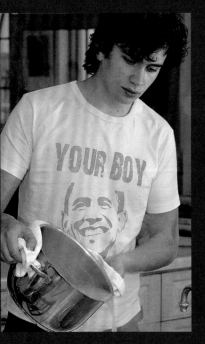

Chop Suey Noodles

Your basic noodle dish. Keep it simple or add extras.

1. Cook noodles in boiling water as pack directs. Drain well. Mix sauce.

2. Prep vegetables with a sharp knife on a flat board.

3. Put wok or pan on to high heat. Add the oils, swirling to coat the pan.

4. Add the ginger and garlic. Scoop and toss for a few seconds with a long spoon.

5. Add onions, beansprouts. Stir-fry for 1 minute.

6. Add noodles, sauce. Stir till heated thoroughly. Pile into bowls. Eat with chopsticks. Enjoy with Chinese green tea.

YOU CAN

✱ add water chestnuts, bamboo shoots, carrot, leek, onion, dried/fresh mushrooms
✱ add mangetout, baby corn, diced de-seeded chilli, shredded red & white cabbage
✱ add iceberg lettuce, pak choi, choy sum, Chinese leaf, broccoli, spinach
✱ add tofu, cashew nuts … and use any noodles
✱ vary sauces and quantities

Noodle Stir-Fry & Egg Roll

Top noodles with egg roll or wok the lot together.

1. Heat non-stick frying pan or wok (add 3 drops oil if not).
2. Beat eggs, salt, pepper. Spoon/pour a quarter of egg into pan. Cook 1 minute. Roll out. Repeat. Slice rolls in strips. Set aside.
3. Mix sauce ingredients. Set aside. Cook noodles. Drain. Set aside.
4. Prep veg with a sharp knife. Heat wok. Add oils.
5. Toss onion and garlic. Fry 1 minute, stirring. Add mushrooms, pak choi. Stir 1 minute. Add beansprouts. Toss till hot.
6. Add noodles and sauce to heat through. Add half egg strips.
7. Serve, topped with remaining egg roll.

YOU CAN

* beat the eggs in a large bowl. Add cooked noodles, sauce, prepped veg of choice. Add to hot wok. Stir-fry till ready.
* add chilli sauce, coriander, sesame seeds
* vegans – at step 1 marinade tofu in sauce. Pan-fry. Substitute for egg roll.

 FEEDS 2   EXPRESS   VEGAN OPT.

2 eggs
Salt and pepper
110g/4oz soba or egg noodles

Sauce

3 tbsps soy sauce
1 tsp sugar
Pinch salt
Squirt tomato ketchup
Dash malt vinegar
1 tsp cornflour

Stir-fry

4 fat cloves garlic
1 onion
A few beansprouts
A few mushrooms
1 head pak choi
2 tbsps vegetable/sunflower oil
1 tsp sesame oil

FEEDS 2–3 **VEGAN OPT.**

200g/7oz dried egg noodles
Mix of sesame and groundnut/veg oil

Sauce

2 tbsps soy sauce
2 tbsps Chinese rice wine
Pinch sugar
1 tbsp veggie oyster/hoisin/plum/
  black bean sauce
100ml/3½ fl oz veg stock/mushroom
  soaking water
1 tbsp cornflour

Stir-fry

175g/6oz fresh shiitake/oyster/
  Chinese mushrooms or handful
  dried black/shiitake mushrooms
  (cover with boiling water and
  soak for 30 minutes)
1 tbsp oil
3 cloves garlic, sliced
A small knob of ginger, grated
1–2 carrots, cut into sticks or
  ribbons
1–2 leeks, white part, finely
  shredded
4 large iceberg lettuce leaves,
  shredded
A few beansprouts
2–4 spring onions, shredded

Mushroom Chow Mein

Dried black fungus and crisp noodles star here.

1. Soak dried mushrooms. Mix sauce ingredients. Prep vegetables.

2. Cook noodles as pack directs. Drain well. Toss to coat in a few drops of sesame/groundnut oil mix.

3. Crisp noodles: either make 4 noodle nests on a baking tray and cook under low grill for 5–10 minutes per side; or pan-fry 5 minutes per side in oil till golden.

4. Meantime, drain and slice dried mushrooms. Heat a wok. Heat remaining oil. Stir-fry garlic and ginger a few seconds.

5. Add the carrots and leeks. Stir-fry 1–2 minutes. Add mushrooms. Stir-fry 1 minute.

6. Add lettuce, beansprouts, spring onions and sauce. Stir as mix thickens. Pile onto noodles. Serve topped with coriander.

YOU CAN

✱ vary vegetables and add finely diced chilli
✱ vegans – use non-egg noodles

Pad Thai

Reminds me of my gap-year travelling.

1. Soak and cook noodles as pack instructs. Drain well.

2. Heat wok. Add 2 tsps oil. Tip egg in, swirling to make a thin omelette. Cook 1 minute or till set. Remove. Roll. Slice into thin strips. Set aside.

3. Mix tamarind (or soy), sugar, lime juice with 1 tbsp water for sauce. Set aside. Dice tofu. Leave it plain or pan-fry it.

4. Reheat wok. Add remaining oil. Stir-fry shallot/onion, garlic, chilli for 30 seconds. Add tofu. Toss for 30 seconds.

5. Add noodles, tamarind sauce. Stir. Add beansprouts. Serve topped with coriander, peanuts, egg strips, soy sauce.

YOU CAN

✱ make Singapore Fried Noodles. Use thin rice vermicelli at step 1. Skip the sauce. At step 4 add ginger to onion etc. At step 5 use 200g/7oz beansprouts. Skip peanuts. Add large pinch curry powder, 2 tbsps soy with noodles. Top with egg strips and coriander or basil.

FEEDS 2   VEGAN OPT.   EXPRESS

200g/7oz dried rice noodles
4 tsps groundnut/sunflower oil
2 eggs, beaten
1 tbsp tamarind paste/soy sauce
1 tbsp brown sugar
Juice of 2 limes
1 shallot/small onion, finely chopped
4 cloves garlic, crushed
Pinch chilli flakes
1 pack tofu (for prep see pg 12)
Handful beansprouts
Lots of coriander, finely chopped
3 tbsps roast peanuts, chopped
Splash soy (if using tamarind)

RICE

Rice isn't just an extra — it needs as much care as the stuff you put with it. See page 12.

FEEDS 1 · VEGAN · EXPRESS

50g/2oz basmati rice, rinsed

Stir-fry

½ tbsp groundnut/sesame oil
1 plump clove garlic, sliced
A little fresh ginger, grated/chopped
A few sprigs/florets tenderstem broccoli
1 head pak choi, trimmed, leaves stripped, sliced
1–2 spring onions, sliced
A few cashew nuts
A little chilli sauce

Sauce

1 tbsp soy sauce
Pinch sugar
1 tbsp rice wine

Asian Veg & Cashew Nuts on Basmati

Shape your rice in a mould to make this look impressive.

1. Boil pan of water. Add rice. Cook 10 minutes or till soft to bite (page 12).
2. Meantime, prepare vegetables. Mix sauce.
3. Drain rice when cooked. Replace in pan. Cover with cloth.
4. Heat a wok. Add oil. Swirl. Stir-fry garlic and ginger until fragrant.
5. Add broccoli. Stir-fry 2 minutes. Add pak choi and spring onion.
6. Stir fry 1 minute. Add sauce, cashew nuts. Stir-fry to heat through.
7. Press rice into a chef's or large cutting ring on a plate. Remove.
8. Top with stir-fry and serve with a few dabs of chilli sauce.

YOU CAN
* add veggie oyster or black bean sauce
* slap on some stir-fried tofu

Thai-Style Tofu, Corn & Green Beans on Sticky Rice

An exciting way with rice and tofu.

1. Tip rice into a pan of boiling water. Cook as pack directs.
2. Meantime prepare and slice tofu (pg 12).
3. Heat at least 5cm/2in oil in wok/deep pan to 170°C/325°F, or till a breadcrumb crisps.
4. Add tofu. Turn till golden. Remove. Drain on paper. Discard oil.
5. Replace 2 tbsps oil. Reheat. Cook garlic briefly without browning. Add curry paste. Stir. Add beans, corn and the sauce.
6. Stir-fry till veg soften. Add tofu, to heat through. Drain rice.
7. Press rice into rings/moulds or tip into bowls. Top with a tower of stir-fry. Add nuts, juice and basil.

FEEDS 1–2 · **VEGAN** · **EXPRESS**

110g/4oz Thai sticky rice (unrinsed)
Half a pack of tofu, sliced into lengths 4x2cm/1½x¾in
Oil for frying
1 tablespoon good red curry paste
Handful green beans
Handful baby corn
2 cloves garlic, finely chopped

Sauce

2 tbsps soy sauce
4 tbsps water

Finishing

Squeeze of lime (or lemon juice)
A few roasted peanuts/cashews, crushed (optional)
Basil leaves

2 tbsps olive oil
1 large onion, finely chopped
2 cloves garlic, crushed
1–2 tsps chilli or pinch chilli flakes, or 1
    red chilli, de-seeded, finely chopped
1 x 400g/14oz can chopped tomatoes
1–2 tbsps tomato purée
Pinch sugar
1 tsp oregano/thyme or freshly
    chopped coriander
1 x 400g/14oz can butter/cannellini
    beans
1 x 400g/14oz can kidney beans
225g/8oz basmati/other long-grain
    rice
A little red onion, diced or sliced
    into rings

Rice & Veggie Chilli

Serve this student classic with any long-grain rice. Eat with guacamole, grated Cheddar, tortillas, sour cream, salsa.

1. Heat oil in a pan. Add onion and cook gently 5 minutes. Add garlic, chilli. Cook 3 minutes. Add tomatoes, purée, sugar, herbs. Boil. Reduce heat. Simmer 10 minutes. Taste.

2. Blitz the sauce till smooth with handblender or leave textured. Add beans. Simmer 10 minutes.

3. Meantime, rinse rice. Add to boiling water. Cook as pack directs. Drain. Return to pan. Cover with a cloth. Fluff with a fork after 3 minutes.

4. Serve rice in bowls topped with chilli and red onion. Or mould in cup, ramekin or ring. Invert onto plate. Top with chilli.

YOU CAN

✳ top chilli with mash. Bake as for Shepherd's Pie (pg 147).

✳ cover with garlic breadcrumbs (pg 103), dot with butter. Bake 20 minutes.

✳ cover with grated Cheddar. Grill till bubbling.

✳ cover with slices of baguette, spread with garlic butter. Bake till crispy.

Red Chilli Aubergine Rice Bowl

Even if you're not keen on aubergine – try this. Everyone I've made it for texts for the recipe.

FEEDS 3

VEGAN

EXPRESS

1. Put choice of rice into a pan of boiling water. Cook as pack directs. Meantime, prepare vegetables and mix sauce ingredients.

2. Heat a wok. Add oil. Swirl to heat. Add the chunks of aubergine. Toss to stir-fry for 5 minutes or until just tender. Remove. You may need to do this in batches.

3. Heat a bit more oil. Add ginger, garlic, chilli, spring onion. Stir-fry briefly without colouring. Add the stock, sauce, aubergines, beansprouts, green leaf, seasoning. Stir to heat through and thicken. Tip onto rice. Add coriander, chopped spring onion, chilli.

YOU CAN

* add a bit more liquid for a saucier stir-fry
* eat on noodles

200g/7oz Thai sticky, unrinsed, or basmati rice, rinsed
2 tbsps groundnut/veg/sunflower oil
½ tbsp sesame oil
2 aubergines, chopped roughly, bite-size
Small knob of ginger, grated
3 cloves garlic, crushed
1 red chilli, de-seeded, sliced thinly
3 spring onions, sliced
125ml veg stock/water
Handful beansprouts
A little Chinese leaf/pak choi, shredded
Salt and pepper
Fresh coriander and/or extra spring onion

Sauce

3 tbsps soy sauce
1 tbsp malt vinegar
1 tbsp brown sugar

FEEDS 3–4

VEGAN OPT.

1.2 litres/2 pints or more
  homemade stock (pg 184)
35g/1½oz butter
½ tbsp olive oil
6–8 shallots, finely chopped
3 fat cloves garlic, crushed
275g/10oz Arborio/Carnaroli/Vialone
  Nano risotto rice (unrinsed)
Fresh tarragon/thyme/rosemary,
  finely chopped
2 carrots, sliced
1 courgette, chopped
A few button/chestnut mushrooms
Juice of ½ lemon
4–6 heaped tbsps Parmesan, plus
  extra for grating at table
Pinch celery salt (optional)
Salt and pepper

Risotto

Use homemade stock and a variety of veg for contrasting textures and deeper flavour – season creatively and pile loads of cheese on.

1. Make stock (pg 184) or defrost frozen. Simmer v gently in a pan.

2. Melt butter, oil in a second pan. Sweat shallots, garlic v gently till softened.

3. Add carrots, sweat 3 minutes. Add a little herb. Raise heat. Throw rice in. Stir constantly for 2–3 minutes. Reduce heat. Add courgette, mushrooms.

4. Add a ladleful of hot stock. Stir, cooking till absorbed. Add another. Repeat, stirring constantly, cooking slowly as rice swells until stock's used and rice is soft (15–20 minutes). Add lemon plus extra stock if needed for thick soupy texture.

5. Add herbs, Parmesan, seasoning, extra butter; taste and adjust.

6. Cover for 3 minutes. Serve in bowls topped with extra herbs, butter, cheese, oil, seasoning.

YOU CAN

✳ make Mixed Mushroom Risotto. At step 1 soak 10g/½oz dried porcini mushrooms in 4 tbsps hot stock/water for 20 minutes. Add the lot at end of step 3 with 350g/12oz chopped chestnut mushrooms.

✳ make Tomato Risotto. Half-way through step 4 add 5 chopped tomatoes and/or sundried tomatoes. Top with basil, olives, optional rocket.

Roasted Butternut Squash Risotto

1. Preheat oven to 200°C/400°F/gas 6.
2. Drizzle squash with oil, salt, garlic. Roast 20 minutes or till soft.
3. Make risotto: skip carrot/mushroom. Add roasted squash at end of step 4, saving a bit for top with herb, spinach wilted in a little butter.

YOU CAN

* make it smooth. Melt 50g/2oz butter in pan. Add chunks of squash. Cook gently for 15 minutes or till soft. Purée with handblender or mash and season. Stir into rice at end of step 4.

FEEDS 3–4   VEGAN OPT.

1 x basic risotto (opposite)

Plus

1 butternut squash, peeled, de-seeded, chopped
Olive oil
Salt
2 cloves garlic, chopped
A little dried sage (optional)
A handful spinach
A little butter

Pea & Lemon Risotto

1. Boil peas, garlic, mint for 2–3 minutes. Drain, reserving water.
2. Blitz or mash half with a bit of hot cooking water.
3. Meantime, make risotto (skip carrot/mushroom). Stir whole and blitzed peas in at end of step 4 with lemon juice and zest to taste. Season. Stir in basil/rocket, grated cheese, optional butter/cream/crème fraîche..

YOU CAN

* add asparagus tips and broad beans

FEEDS 3–4   VEGAN OPT.

1 x basic risotto (opposite)

Plus

200g/7oz fresh/ frozen peas
1 clove garlic
A few fresh mint leaves
½–1 lemon, zest and juice
Salt and pepper
Fresh basil/rocket
Bit of Parmesan/Lancashire/Cheddar, grated
Extra butter/1 tbsp cream/crème fraîche (optional)

BURGERS

Sometimes only a burger will do. Cook inside or slap on the barbie. Mix it up with stackings and relishes.

MAKES 6 **EXPRESS**

Chips

900g/2lb old potatoes, scrubbed
2 tbsps olive oil
Salt

Burgers

1 x 400g/ 14oz can black-eyed beans
1 small red onion, finely chopped
75g/3oz Cheddar, grated
75g/3oz fresh breadcrumbs (pg 12)
1 clove garlic, crushed
1 tsp smoked paprika
½ beaten egg if needed
Fresh coriander or dried oregano/ thyme
2 shakes Tabasco or pinch chilli
Salt and pepper
Flour for shaping
Oil for frying

Bread rolls

Stackers

Shredded iceberg lettuce, grated Cheddar, sliced tomato, sliced cucumber, cucumber pickle (pg 185), chutney, dill pickle, mayo, ketchup, chilli jam, sliced avocado, guacamole (pg 52), onion rings (pg 161), raita (pg 57), tzatziki (pg 53), hummus (pg 55)

Smoky Burgers & Chips
Barbecue flavoured by smoked paprika.

1. Chips: Preheat oven to 200°C/400°F/gas 6. Scrub spuds. Dry. Chop into wedges. Dry again. Roll in oil and salt or tip everything into a freezer bag and shake. Bake on a tray for 30 minutes or till crisp and golden.

2. Burgers: mash drained beans roughly with a fork. Add everything else. Mix well. Shape into 4–6 burgers with floured hands.

3. Fry gently in hot oil 5 minutes per side till crisp and cooked.

4. Sit in warm or griddled rolls with choice of relishes and stacking ingredients.

YOU CAN
✱ make sweet-potato chips. Peel, then roll in sunflower oil, salt. Bake 20 minutes till caramelized.

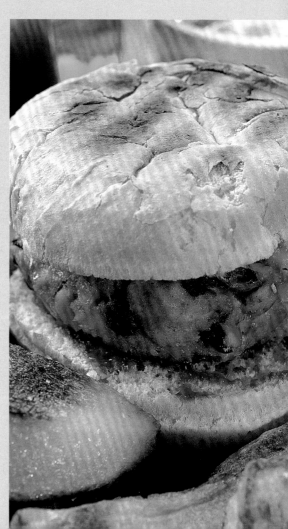

MAKES 6 · VEGAN · EXPRESS

110g/4oz onion, finely chopped
2 cloves garlic, crushed
3 tbsps olive oil
1 small dried chilli, crumbled
1 tsp ground cumin
1 tsp ground coriander
¼ tsp turmeric
1 tsp lemon grass paste or ½ stalk, very finely chopped
200g/7oz chestnut mushrooms, finely chopped
Juice of 1 lime
1 x 400g/14oz can chickpeas
75g/3oz fresh breadcrumbs (pg 12)
A few shakes Tabasco
2 tbsps fresh coriander
Salt and pepper
Flour for coating
Oil for frying

Bread rolls
Stackers (pg 124)

Mushroom & Chickpea Burgers

Cracking tastes and textures – balanced for protein.

1. Gently fry onion and garlic in hot oil, stirring for 5 minutes or until soft.

2. Add chilli, cumin, coriander, turmeric, lemon grass. Cook for 3 minutes.

3. Add mushroom, lime. Cook 5 minutes to soften. Tip mix into bowl to cool.

4. Semi-blitz drained chickpeas with a handblender/processor or crush with a fork, but don't turn to paste. Add to cooling mix with breadcrumbs, Tabasco, coriander, salt and pepper.

5. Scatter flour onto a plate and coat hands. Shape mix gently into 6, washing hands, re-flouring. Chill. Fry in oil for 5 minutes per side or till cooked through. Serve in rolls with choice of stackers.

YOU CAN
* stack with curry mayo, raita, spinach, coriander, mango chutney
* top with an onion ring (pg 161) and fried whole chilli

110g/4oz fresh breadcrumbs (pg 12)
175g/6oz Lancashire cheese, grated
1 medium onion, finely chopped
2 tbsps gram flour
1–2 tbsps fresh mint or basil/dill/
    parsley/coriander
1 large egg
1 tsp English mustard
Lemon rind
Salt and pepper
Sunflower/vegetable oil for frying

Bread rolls
Stackers (pg 124)

Lancashire Burgers

A very British burger – the cheese does it.

1. Tip all the ingredients into a bowl.

2. Mix with a fork. Chill in the fridge till needed, for easier handling.

3. Divide the mix into 6 flat burgers. Heat oil in a pan. Fry gently for 4 minutes per side or till cooked through and golden. Serve in rolls with choice of stackers.

YOU CAN
* stack with apple chutney/pickle, sliced apple, onion rings (pg 161)
* make Chilli Cheese Burger – add a diced red chilli

Red Bean Burgers

Couldn't be healthier, easier, tastier.

1. Drain beans. Tip onto board. Chop roughly.
2. Blitz bread to crumbs (pg 12). Mix everything with a fork.
3. Shape into 8. Coat lightly in flour. Chill or cook now.
4. Heat oil in a pan. Cook gently 5 minutes per side or till cooked through. Slap between rolls, stacked.

YOU CAN
* use dried beans. Soak and cook 150g/5oz of each type (pg 13).
* eat with coleslaw (pg 73)

MAKES 8 | VEGAN OPT. | EXPRESS

1 x 400g/14oz can cannellini beans
1 x 400g/14oz can red kidney beans
110g/4oz white bread
25g/1oz grated Cheddar
1 small carrot, grated
3 cloves garlic, crushed
2 tbsps fresh coriander, finely chopped
½ tsp chilli powder
2 tsps cumin
¼ tsp cinnamon
2 tbsps tomato purée
Salt and pepper
White flour for coating
Olive/sunflower/veg/groundnut oil
   for frying

Bread rolls
Stackers (pg 124)

Falafel Burgers

Ultimate Gastonbury-style burger (or pittas).

1. Drain chickpeas. Dry on paper. Blitz bread to crumbs (pg 12).
2. Add chickpeas, onion, garlic, spices, herbs, seasoning. Blitz to a paste in a processor/with a handblender or mix with a fork.
3. Shape large tablespoons of mix into small burgers. Roll lightly in flour to prevent dissolving. Chill if you have time.
4. Pour oil into a small pan – at least 1cm/½in deep. Heat. Shallow-fry gently for 2–3 minutes till lightly browned. Turn gently. Fry till golden and cooked through. Stack in rolls or stuff pittas.

YOU CAN
* coat burgers in flour, beaten egg, breadcrumbs before frying
* stack with Hummus, Baba Ganoush, Tahini (all pg 55), Greek salad (pg 72)

MAKES 10 | VEGAN | EXPRESS

1 x 400g/14oz can chickpeas
50g/2oz white bread
1 medium onion, roughly chopped
4–5 cloves garlic, peeled
2 tsps ground coriander
2 tsps ground cumin
1 tsp chilli powder
2 tbsps fresh coriander, chopped
Salt and pepper
White flour for coating
Sunflower/groundnut oil for frying

Bread rolls
Stackers (pg 124)

FEEDS 4 VEGAN

3 large potatoes
1 large sweet potato
2 tbsps sunflower/groundnut oil
1 large onion, finely chopped
4 cloves garlic, crushed
Pinch salt
2 tbsps korma curry paste
1 x 400g/14oz can chickpeas (or
    150g dried, cooked)
500ml/18fl oz water/veg stock
Juice of 1 lemon
1 x 200ml/7fl oz carton coconut
    cream
1 tbsp mango chutney
1 tbsp tomato purée
4 tbsps chopped coriander leaves
1 x 200g/7oz can chopped tomatoes
2 tbsps ground almonds (optional)
Handful spinach

Chickpea, Spinach & Potato Curry

1. Peel all potatoes. Cut them into bite-sized chunks. Heat oil in a large pan or casserole dish.

2. Add the onion, garlic, pinch of salt. Cook gently over a low heat for five minutes until soft, not coloured.

3. Stir in curry paste. Cook 2 minutes, stirring. Add the potatoes, chickpeas. Stir for 1 minute.

4. Add remaining ingredients except spinach. Bring to the boil. Stir. Reduce heat to low. Cover.

5. Simmer gently for 45 minutes, stirring occasionally. Add the spinach 2 minutes before you're ready to eat. Serve with rice or scoop with chapattis (pg 129).

YOU CAN
* use butternut squash. Add other vegetables and beans.
* eat with yogurt or raita (pg 57), naan or poppadoms

Tikka Masala Dahl

1. Tip lentils into a sieve. Rinse under a tap. Drain well.

2. Fry onion gently in hot oil in a large pan till soft. Add garlic, chilli, curry paste. Stir 2 minutes. Stir lentils in.

3. Dissolve creamed coconut in hot water. Add purée and chutney. Add to lentils with ½ lemon, cinnamon.

4. Stir. Simmer gently 15 minutes. Add a splash of water if dry – it should be soft, creamy, thick. Taste and season with lemon, salt, fresh coriander. Spoon onto plates or scoop with chapattis.

YOU CAN

✱ top with fried garlic slices, popped cumin and onion seed

✱ add bits of potato/sweet potato/cauliflower/ginger, green beans, peas, hard-boiled egg

✱ make Chapattis. Sift 225g/8oz chapatti/white/wholemeal & white flour with ½tsp salt. Work in 175ml/6fl oz water with hands. Knead 7 minutes. Leave, covered, 10 minutes. Roll small bits out very thinly into circles. Cook in dry pan, a few seconds per side.

 FEEDS 2 VEGAN EXPRESS

225g/8oz red lentils
2 tbsps groundnut/sunflower oil
1 large onion, chopped finely
4 cloves garlic, crushed
½–1 green chilli, de-seeded, finely chopped
2 tbsps tikka masala paste
110g/4oz creamed coconut
1 litre/1¾ pints hot water
2 tbsps tomato purée
1 tbsp mango chutney
1 lemon
1 cinnamon stick (optional)
Salt
Large bunch fresh coriander, chopped

2 tbsps groundnut/sunflower oil
1 tsp black mustard seeds
1 very large onion
6 fresh/4 dried curry leaves
2.5cm/1in ginger, peeled, grated
1 tsp turmeric
1–2 medium green chillies, de-
  seeded, finely chopped
450g/1lb peeled waxy potatoes (e.g.
  Charlotte/salad/new) or floury
  type (Maris Piper, King Edward)
300–350ml/10–12fl oz water
Handful baby spinach, chopped
Juice of ½ lemon/2 tsps tamarind
  paste
Pinch salt

Bombay Aloo

1. Heat oil in frying pan. Add seeds. Cover to pop. Add onions, curry leaves, ginger, turmeric, chillies. Cook gently till soft (10 minutes.)

2. Add potatoes. Cook and stir 1 minute. Add water. Boil. Reduce heat and cook extremely gently for 10 minutes plus, till potatoes are soft and coated in thick sauce. Add a splash of water if too dry.

3. Add spinach, tamarind/lemon, salt and cook till spinach wilted. Eat with chapattis (pg 129) or as a side dish.

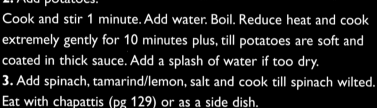

YOU CAN
* add mushrooms, peas, chopped okra, garlic
* add chopped tomatoes, cream, coriander

225g/8oz white bread flour
Good pinch salt
1 x 7g/¼oz sachet dried fast action
  yeast
Pinch black onion seeds
4–6 tbsps warm milk
1 tbsp vegetable/groundnut oil
3 tbsps natural yogurt
Melted butter for brushing

Naan Bread

1. Sift flour and salt into a bowl. Add yeast, onion seeds, milk, oil, yogurt.

2. Mix to a soft elastic ball of dough with your fingers.

3. Knead (pg 11) on a lightly floured board for 10 minutes.

4. Cover. Leave in a warm place 1 hour or till doubled in volume.

5. Preheat oven to 230°C/425°F/gas 8. Knead dough for 2 minutes.

6. Divide into 4. Roll into teardrop shapes. Sit on greased trays.

7. Cook 4 minutes or till puffy. Grill naan a few seconds till just browned. Brush with melted butter and extra seeds. Eat now.

YOU CAN
* add chopped garlic, fresh coriander at step 5

Lemon Spiced Rice

1. Wash rice or soak in cold water for 30 minutes. Drain. Dry.
2. Heat oil in pan on low heat. Add spices. Cook for 2 minutes.
3. Add rice. Stir for 1 minute. Add juice. Add boiling water.
4. Stir once. Cover. Cook on extremely low heat for 10 minutes.
5. Remove. Leave for 5 minutes. Fluff rice with a fork. Serve.

YOU CAN

✱ fry up an onion till soft at step 2 before adding spices

Paneer Tikka Skewers

1. Mix coating in a bowl. Add cheese and veg. Leave 30 minutes.
2. Meantime, soak wooden skewers in cold water.
3. Preheat grill. Thread cheese and veg onto skewers.
4. Brush with oil/melted butter. Grill, turning regularly, till cheese is golden and veg softening. Serve with lemon for squeezing.

YOU CAN

✱ wrap in tortillas with chutney, raita, salad
✱ vary veg – add mushrooms, courgettes. Vegans – skip cheeses, use tofu.

FEEDS 4 · **VEGAN** · **EXPRESS**

350g/12oz basmati rice
2 tbsps groundnut/sunflower oil
4 cloves
5 cardamom pods, bashed
Small cinnamon stick
1–2 bay leaves
Pinch cumin/black onion seeds (optional)
2 tbsps lemon juice
600ml/1 pint boiling water

FEEDS 3–4 · **VEGAN OPT.**

1 block paneer cheese, cut into bite-size bits
2 red onions
3 red peppers

Coating

5 tbsps plain yogurt
2 tsps cornflour
2 tsps sunflower/vegetable oil
4 cloves garlic, crushed
5cm/2in peeled ginger, grated
Pinch salt
1 tsp chilli powder
1 tsp garam masala
Pinch ground cumin
2 tbsps lemon juice
2 tbsps Cheddar, grated
Extra oil/melted butter for cooking
Lemon chunks for serving

1 v large peeled onion, v thinly sliced
1–2 tbsps olive oil
1.2 litres/2 pints water
225g/8oz brown lentils
50g/2oz basmati/long-grain rice
Salt and pepper

Lentils, Rice & Sticky Onions

Simple, low-cost, absolutely delicious.

1. Fry onion gently in oil in a frying pan over a very low heat, 20–30 minutes, till caramelized (don't burn it). Set aside.

2. Meantime, boil the water in a pan and add the lentils. Cook 20 minutes or till tender, still with bite.

3. Add rinsed rice. Cook 10 minutes or till rice is tender. Drain off any excess water. Cover for 5 minutes. Tip onto a plate.

4. Stir in half the onions and seasoning using a fork. Pile the rest on top.

YOU CAN

✱ use green lentils or quinoa but add the rice earlier as both cook quickly

✱ eat with griddled veg/halloumi/hummus (pg 55), olives, tzatziki (pg 53), hard boiled egg, yogurt, watercress, tomato and onion salad (pg 72)

FEEDS 4

VEGAN

2–3 tbsps olive/vegetable oil
1 large onion, finely chopped
3–4 cloves garlic, crushed
1 tsp ground cumin
1 tsp ground ginger
1 tsp ground turmeric
1 fresh chilli, de-seeded, finely
   chopped, or ½ tsp chilli flakes
1 aubergine, chopped into bite-size
   chunks
1 x 400g/14oz can tomatoes
300ml/10fl oz water or water plus
   passata
1 x 400g/14oz can chickpeas
6 dried apricots, chopped
1–2 tbsps tomato purée
175g/6oz butternut squash, cubed
175g/6oz parsnips, cubed
1 large carrot, sliced
1 tsp sugar/honey
Good squeeze lemon juice
Salt and pepper

Couscous

180–225g/6–8oz couscous
Boiling water
Fresh coriander

Moroccan Veg & Chickpea Tagine

Fine spicy, North African stew. Slam it on the table and everyone get in there.

1. Heat oil in a large pan. Cook onion gently in a large pan for 5–10 minutes. Add garlic, spices, chilli/flakes. Stir for 1 minute. Add more oil. Add aubergine. Stir 2–3 minutes.

2. Add tomatoes, water, chickpeas, apricots, purée. Boil and stir then simmer gently on low heat for 15 minutes. Add squash, parsnips, carrot, honey, lemon, seasoning.

3. Boil then reduce heat. Simmer 20–30 minutes until veg are tender but hold shape, and you have a thick sauce. Add more water/purée if needed. Season. Taste. Adjust.

4. Pour boiling water over couscous. Cover. Leave 5 minutes. Fluff it up with a fork. Season well. Serve with the tagine and coriander.

YOU CAN
* top with flaked almonds, add raisins
* add 2–3 tsps harissa paste for extra bite
* serve with quinoa for complete protein

STUFFED VEG PLATE

Veggie clichés maybe, but this lot taste special. Experiment with herbs, spices, new flavours and textures.

FEEDS 4 **VEGAN OPT.**

2 large red peppers
2 large yellow peppers
Crushed garlic
4 tbsps olive oil
Salt and pepper
16 cherry tomatoes, halved
50g/2oz feta cheese
4 cloves garlic, sliced
A few black olives
4 cloves garlic, whole
Chunks of lemon
Fresh basil

FEEDS 2 **VEGAN OPT.**

4 beef or other large tomatoes
Salt
1 clove garlic, crushed

Filling

60g/2½oz risotto rice
25g/1oz butter
Grated lemon rind
50g/2oz grated cheese
Finely chopped herbs
Salt and pepper

Peppers

1. Preheat oven to 200°C/400°F/gas 6. Halve peppers lengthways. Spoon out seeds and core. Rub crushed garlic round the insides.
2. Brush or roll the outsides in oil. Sit halves side by side in a lightly oiled dish. Season. Place 2 cherry tomato halves in each pepper.
3. Top with crumbled feta, sliced garlic, olives. Drizzle with oil. Drop whole garlic cloves in dish with lemon, basil. Cook, foil-covered, for 20 minutes. Uncover. Cook a further 10 minutes or till tender.

YOU CAN
* steep tomatoes in boiling water 1 minute, then peel skins off
* stuff with cooked couscous, cheese, mushrooms – bake
* stuff with diced cooked potatoes, cumin, yogurt, coriander – bake
* stuff with crumbled goat's cheese, onion, grated lemon – bake

Tomatoes

1. Slice tops off tomatoes at stem end. Save lids.
2. Hollow out carefully using sharp knife and spoon.
3. Roughly chop the flesh to use later.
4. Rub salt and garlic round the insides. Invert. Leave 30 minutes to drain excess moisture. Preheat oven to 200°C/400°F/gas 6.
5. Boil rice for 10 minutes in lightly salted water till half-cooked. Drain. Mix with butter, lemon rind, cheese, herbs, chopped tomato flesh, seasoning.
6. Stuff mix into shells. Top with lids. Drizzle a little oil. Bake 25–30 minutes.

YOU CAN
* fill with breadcrumb mix (see opposite) or omit cheese for vegans
* crack an egg into seasoned tomato. Top with cream/garlic/tomato purée mix. Bake 15 minutes or until just set.

Aubergines

1. Preheat oven to 200°C/400°F/gas 6. Cut aubergines in half lengthways. Criss-cross cut surface with a sharp knife.
2. Brush with a bit of oil. Cook on a baking tray till tender (20–30 minutes). Remove flesh with care, leaving shells intact.
3. Heat butter in oil and lightly fry onion, garlic till soft. Add mushrooms. Fry lightly. Add chopped aubergine flesh. Fry 2 minutes. Tip mix into bowl with crumbs, pinenuts, lemon rind, paprika, salt, pepper, herb. Stuff shells. Sprinkle oil. Bake 15 minutes.

YOU CAN
* add a few raisins, pinch cinnamon
* beat an egg into the mix

FEEDS 2   VEGAN

2 aubergines
1 tbsp oil/½oz butter
1 small onion, finely chopped
2 cloves garlic, crushed
4 white mushrooms, diced
4–6 tsps white breadcrumbs (pg 12)
Pinenuts
A little lemon rind
Paprika
Salt and pepper
Parsley/mint

135

FEEDS 4

1 large onion, finely chopped
3 fat cloves garlic, crushed
1–2 tbsps olive oil
450g/1lb baby spinach or regular,
 washed, dried, tough stalks
 removed
350g/12oz feta cheese
Handful pinenuts
Grated fresh nutmeg
Salt and pepper
25–50g/1–2oz melted butter
1 pack filo pastry (12–16 sheets)
Poppy or sesame seeds (optional)

Spanakopita

Crisp filo pastry wraps a beautiful soft cheese and spinach filling. This is deceptively easy and tastes awesome.

1. Preheat oven to 230°C/450°F/gas 8.

2. Filling: cook onion, garlic gently in oil in a large pan for 5 minutes. Add spinach. Stir to wilt for 4 minutes. Drain/squeeze thoroughly. Mix in a bowl with feta, pinenuts, nutmeg, seasoning. Set aside.

3. Base: brush interior of a 23cm/9in loose-bottomed tart tin with melted butter. Lay one sheet of filo across it, leaving edges hanging over. Brush with butter. Lay second sheet over for a cross shape. Brush again. Repeat, crossing and buttering at different angles, till 6–8 sheets used and base is covered. Add filling.

4. Top it: repeat sequence of laying filo across, one sheet at a time, buttering as you go, but roll the edges in and tuck them down to seal the pie. Continue till the top is covered. Remove rim from tin.

5. Sit tart on base onto a baking tray. Brush top with butter, seeds.

6. Bake 15–20 minutes till crisp and golden. Eat hot, warm, cold.

3 courgettes, chunked
3 red onions, quartered
4–6 tomatoes, halved/quartered
A few button mushrooms, de-stalked
Bay leaves (optional)
2 x 250g/9oz packs halloumi cheese

Marinade

3 tbsps olive oil
2 fat cloves garlic, crushed
Juice of 1 lemon
Dried thyme/oregano or fresh herbs of choice
Salt and pepper

Pilaf

2 tbsps oil
1 onion, finely chopped
4 cardamom pods
½ tsp each turmeric, cinnamon
225g/8oz basmati/long grain rice
350ml/12fl oz veg stock/water
Fresh coriander/parsley

Veg & Halloumi Skewers on Pilaf

Slap on the barbie or grill inside – team with pilaf, bulgur, couscous or quinoa for top taste and nutrition.

1. Skewers: tip mixed marinade into bowl with veg, bay leaves if using, cubed halloumi. Leave 30 minutes while soaking wooden skewers in cold water (or use metal ones).

2. Pilaf: heat oil in large pan. Fry onion gently till soft, golden brown. Add cardamom, turmeric, cinnamon. Cook 2 minutes.

3. Add washed rice. Stir 1 minute. Add stock. Boil. Reduce to very low heat for 10 minutes or till tender. Remove. Set aside, covered.

4. Thread veg, halloumi onto skewers. Cook under preheated grill, turning regularly, brushing with marinade, till cheese is soft, veg still crisp. Serve on fork-fluffed pilau, topped with coriander/parsley.

YOU CAN

✱ add chopped, dried apricots to cooking rice. Top with flaked almonds/pinenuts.

✱ serve de-skewered cheese and veg in flatbreads/pittas, on couscous (pg 133) or bulgur (pg 13)

✱ skip cheese: use marinated tofu or just veg

 FEEDS 4

 VEGAN OPT.

2 large floury potatoes, peeled
Olive oil
1 large onion, finely chopped
3 cloves garlic, crushed
2 x 400g/14oz cans tomatoes
Splash of mushroom ketchup
Squeeze of lemon juice
A good pinch of sugar
1 tsp dried/fresh oregano
Pinch cinnamon
2 tbsps tomato purée
1 x 400g/14oz can kidney beans
2 tbsps fresh parsley, chopped
Salt and pepper
2 aubergines, sliced
1 x cheese sauce (pg 110)

Moussaka

Enjoy this bubbly, cheesy Greek classic that makes the most of aubergines. Tastes gorgeous.

1. Boil potatoes till just tender. Drain. Slice.

2. Meantime, fry onion, garlic gently in oil in a large pan for 5 minutes till soft. Add tomatoes, ketchup, lemon juice, oregano, sugar, purée. Boil. Reduce heat. Simmer 10 minutes. Add beans. Simmer 20 minutes. Taste, add parsley, seasoning. Add 1 tbsp cheese sauce when done.

3. Meantime, fry aubergine slices in 2–3 tbsps oil, turning, till soft, or griddle. Drain on kitchen paper.

4. Make cheese sauce (pg 110). Preheat oven to 190°C/375°F/gas 5.

5. Grease a large ovenproof dish or 4 small ones. Layer tomato/bean mix, aubergine, grated cheese, drizzle of sauce, potato slices. Repeat, finishing with aubergine, cheese sauce. Bake 1 hour. Rest 10 minutes. Good with Tomato & Onion or Greek salad (pg 72).

YOU CAN
* layer in cooked macaroni. Vegans, top with plain sauce or breadcrumbs.

Aubergine Parmigiana

A sophisticated Italian way with aubergine. Enjoy with ciabatta, salad.

FEEDS
4

1. Preheat oven to 220°C/425°F/gas 7. Drizzle oil over baking tray.
2. Slice aubergines in 5mm/¼ in-thick circles. Brush with more oil. Scatter basil. Bake 10 minutes (or griddle (pg 48) till tender).
3. Prepare tomato sauce (pg 106) and heat.
4. Grease a shallow dish. Layer tomato sauce, cheese, aubergine.
5. Finish with aubergine, then cheese. Bake 15 minutes or till bubbling hot.

Olive oil
2 large aubergines
Basil leaves
1 x garlicky tomato sauce (pg 106) or 1 bottle passata with garlic
175–225g/6–8oz mixed Cheddar, mozzarella, Parmesan, grated

YOU CAN
✱ make Aubergine Roll-ups. Cut 2 large aubergines lengthways into 5 or 6. Coat in flour, beaten egg. Fry 1–2 minutes per side. Season. Top with basil, grated halloumi/ mozzarella. Roll up. Bake 20 minutes on tomato sauce, topped with mozzarella/ Cheddar.

2 packs tofu, in strips, or 4
portobello mushrooms, sliced, or
Quorn bits
1 courgette, in ribbons or thin strips

Marinade

Fajitas

Mexican street food – perfect for the sofa. Chilli up the

Burritos

Great crowd-pleasers and so easy.

1. Grease an ovenproof dish. Preheat oven to 220°C/425°C/gas 7.
2. Drain beans. Mix with half tomato sauce, optional jalapeños.
3. Lay out tortillas. Spread with sour cream, bean mix, half Cheddar, onions.
4. Fold 2 sides in, then the ends to make parcels. Place seam down in dish. Cover with foil. Bake 15–20 minutes. Preheat grill to medium.
5. Remove foil from dish. Spread with remaining sauce and Cheddar. Grill till bubbling. Eat with guacamole, sour cream, green salad.

YOU CAN
* fill with re-fried or black beans and seasoned passata with crushed garlic
* fill with lightly fried chunks of courgette, tomato sauce, Cheddar, oregano
* fix burritos with cocktail sticks. Fry till golden/cooked through.
* fold filled burrito as omelette. Brush with oil. Bake 10 minutes uncovered. Top with a fried egg, eat with spicy tomato sauce/salsa etc.
* use chickpeas, black-eyed, kidney or black beans

1 x 400g/14oz can borlotti beans or 150g/5oz dried, cooked (pg 12)
1 tomato sauce (pg 106) with added chilli flakes or fresh chilli
A few pickled jalapeños (optional)
4 tortillas
Sour cream
Grated Cheddar
1 small red onion, thinly sliced
Guacamole (pg 52) for serving

3 eggs, beaten
2 tsps mustard
250g/9oz fresh white breadcrumbs
  (pg 12)
1 leek, white part, finely chopped
1 shallot/small onion, chopped
3 cloves garlic, crushed
1 tbsp dill/coriander/parsley,
  chopped
175g/6oz strong cheese e.g. Cheddar,
  Gruyère, Linconshire, grated
Grated rind and juice of ½ lemon
3 tbsps milk
Salt and pepper
A little melted butter for grilling

Top Veggie Sausages

Best veggie sausages. Team with a sharp beetroot salad.

1. Mix eggs and mustard on a plate. Tip two-thirds of the crumbs into a bowl with remaining ingredients. Mix to a stiff paste using two-thirds of the egg mix (add more milk if needed).

2. Roll/shape into 8 sausages. Coat in remaining egg mix, then crumbs. Preheat grill to medium.

3. Brush sausages carefully with butter. Cook on foil-covered rack, turning regularly, for 10 minutes or till melting inside, crisp and golden outside.

YOU CAN

* make Walnut & Beetroot salad. Roast beetroot in foil till cooked or buy a pack. Cube it. Marinate in Honey Mustard Dressing (pg 187). Add 25g/1oz crushed nuts just before serving.

* eat with chilli jam/sweet chilli sauce, watercress, salad

Individual Toad in the Hole

Make this tasty classic with chilled (not frozen) sausages to get the Yorkshires rising. Best with creamy mash, onion gravy (pg 184), garlic stir-fried cabbage.

FEEDS 4

1. Slice sausages. Roll in a mix of ketchup, mustard, onions.

2. Start batter: beat or whisk eggs, milk, salt till frothy. Rest 20 minutes. Preheat oven to 220°C/425°F/gas 7.

3. Put a bit of oil into two 4-hole Yorkshire pudding trays. Heat 5 minutes.

4. Either: beat flour into batter with handblender/whisk. **Or:** sift flour into bowl. Beat the batter in slowly with a wooden spoon.

5. Put a few bits of sausage into each hole in the tin. Fill with batter. Cook 20 minutes plus (don't open the door) until high and delicious.

YOU CAN

✴ cook one big tin (30x20x7cm/12x8x3in). At step 3, heat oil with rosemary, red onion chunks. At step 5 add batter, sausage chunks. Cook 30 minutes plus.

✴ use chunks of butternut squash/red onion/grilled portobello mushroom

1 pack veggie sausages – chilled, not frozen
2 tbsps tomato ketchup
A little mustard
2 spring onions, thinly sliced

Batter

4 eggs
300ml/½ pint milk or milk/water mix
Salt and pepper
225g/8oz plain flour
Oil for baking

1 x pancake batter (pg 34)
1 x cheese sauce (pg 110)
Butter/oil
450g/1lb mixed mushrooms, wiped,
   cut into bite-size chunks/slices
2 cloves garlic, crushed
Fresh or dried parsley/thyme/
   tarragon
Salt and pepper
Extra grated cheese

Mushroom-Stuffed Pancakes

Wonderfully tasty comfort food…

1. Make pancake batter. Make cheese sauce. Set aside.

2. Fry the pancakes (pg 34). Stack them between foil/greaseproof.

3. Heat butter/oil in a pan. Lightly fry mushrooms and garlic. Add herbs and season. Set aside.

4. Preheat oven to 200°C/400°F/gas 6. Grease a shallow ovenproof dish.

5. Lay pancakes out. Grate a little cheese on each one. Place mushroom filling in centre with a dab of sauce. Roll and place in dish. Cover with cheese sauce, extra cheese. Bake 30 minutes till bubbling.

YOU CAN

✳ make pancakes with half wholemeal, half white flour

✳ stuff with beans/chickpeas/Puy lentils in garlicky tomato sauce

✳ speed it up. Sit pancakes on tomato sauce. Brush with butter. Scatter grated cheese. Grill till hot and bubbling.

✳ freeze pancakes, layered with greaseproof

Quick Stuffed Crêpes

A lighter, fast option…

1. Prepare crêpes as pancakes (pg 34), adding poppy seeds.

2. Cook and stack between pieces of greaseproof paper.

3. Preheat oven to 220°C/425°F/gas 7. Grease a baking tray.

4. Prepare filling of choice (below) or improvise.

5. Lay first crêpe out. Pile filling into a corner. Fold in half. Fold again to make a triangle. Lift onto baking tray.

6. Repeat with same or different fillings. Brush with butter. Bake 10 minutes or till cooked through, crisp and bubbling.

FREESTYLE FILLINGS

✱ chickpeas tossed in fried onion, garlic, a little curry paste, coriander, smear of mango chutney

✱ tomato sauce with garlic, mozzarella, fresh basil

✱ spinach wilted in butter/water, crème fraîche, crushed garlic, Cheddar

✱ mushrooms sautéed in butter, garlic, tarragon, crème fraîche

✱ tofu, hoisin sauce, spring onion, beansprouts, garlic, ginger fried in oil 3 minutes. Smear more hoisin.

✱ asparagus spears (pg 107), lemon, butter, garlic, grated cheese

 MAKES 8   EXPRESS   VEGAN OPT.

175g/6oz plain flour
Pinch salt
2 eggs plus 1 yolk
425ml/¾ pint milk
2 tsps melted butter
2 tsps poppy seeds

Freestyle filling (see left)

**FEEDS
4**

Shortcrust pastry

225g/8oz plain white flour
Pinch salt
110g/4oz cold butter
2–3 tbsps very cold water
Beaten egg/milk

Filling

175g/6oz each potato, swede, onion,
 diced small
Oil for frying
A little Vegemite/milk or cream mix
 or veg stock
Seasoning
Fresh/dried herbs
2 tbsps cheese, grated (optional)

Cornish Pasties

You can't beat a good pasty.

1. Make pastry (pg 178). Chill 30 minutes. Preheat oven to 200°C/400°F/gas 6.

2. Fry vegetables very lightly in a little oil for 4 minutes. Add a drizzle of Vegemite/milk or cream or veg stock, seasoning, herbs, optional cheese. Set aside to cool a little.

3. Cut pastry in 4. Roll into squares on a lightly floured board. Cut four 15cm/6in circles using a plate as a template (or guess it). Pile veg onto circles.

4. Dampen edges with water. Pull opposite sides up. Crimp firmly together. Brush with beaten egg/milk while on greased baking tray.

5. Cook 15 minutes. Reduce heat to 190°C/375°F/gas 5. Cook another 15 minutes. Eat warm/hot/to go.

YOU CAN
* stir in 2 tsps curry paste
* fill with chilli (pg 120), Cauliflower Cheese (pg 158), beans and sausage
* make Ch'onion Pasties. Cook 450g/1lb diced onions in butter/oil till soft. Add 170g/6oz diced potato, pinch dried herbs and cook for a further 3 minutes. Cool. Add 450g/1lb grated Cheddar. Prep a pack of all-butter puff pastry as above. Add filling. Bake.

Shepherd's Pie

Keep your carrots chunky to keep it nice and textured.

1. Gently fry onion, garlic in hot oil for 5 minutes till soft. Add carrot, thyme, chilli flakes. Cook 4 minutes. Add tomatoes, lemon juice, sugar, oregano, purée, stock. Simmer gently for 10 minutes. Add beans, cinnamon, relish. Simmer 10 minutes. Taste and season. Preheat oven to 200°C/400°F/gas 6.

2. Make basic mash (pg **162**) using half the cheese. Tip pie mix into one large or individual dishes. Top with mash. Sprinkle remaining cheese. Bake 20–30 minutes.

YOU CAN

✱ add a little diced aubergine, mushroom or cooked lentils

✱ skip cheese. Use non-dairy spread. Add Vegemite to mash.

1 tbsp olive oil
1 large onion, finely chopped
2–3 cloves garlic, crushed
2 carrots, chopped
Pinch dried thyme
Pinch chilli flakes
1 x 400g/14oz can chopped
   tomatoes
Squeeze lemon juice
Pinch sugar
Pinch dried oregano
1 tbsp tomato purée
100ml/3½fl oz veg stock/water
1 x 400g/14oz can mixed beans/
   beans/chickpeas
Pinch cinnamon
Splash Henderson's Relish
Salt and pepper
900g–1.35kg/2–3lb potatoes (mix
   old, white and sweet)
1 tbsp butter
75g/3oz strong Cheddar

MAKES 1

Pastry

175g/6oz plain flour
Pinch salt
110g/4oz cold butter
1 egg yolk
1–2 tbsps cold water

Filling

1 tbsp olive oil
1 tbsp butter
3 big onions (about 700g/1½lb),
  thinly sliced
2 cloves garlic, crushed
3 eggs, plus one yolk, beaten
200ml/7fl oz double cream
75g/3oz Cheddar/Gruyère, grated
Salt and pepper

French Onion Tart

Crumbly pastry and sweet onion filling – people always come back for another slice … or two.

1. Pastry: follow method on pg 178 but add an egg yolk with the water. Chill. Grease a 23cm/9in loose-based tart tin or 4–6 tartlet tins.

2. Roll pastry out very thinly on floured surface to fit base and sides of tin. Lift pastry over on rolling pin. Fit to the tin, repair any tears and finish it (pg 11). Chill 30 minutes. Preheat oven to 180°C/350°F/gas 4.

3. Line tin with baking paper filled with baking beans. Bake 15 minutes. Remove paper/beans. Brush with beaten egg. Bake 2 minutes. Remove.

4. Filling: heat oil and butter in a large pan over low heat. Add onions, garlic. Cover and cook for 15 minutes or till very soft and pale gold.

5. Mix eggs, cream, cheese, seasoning. Add cooled onions. Pour into pastry.

6. Cook 20 minutes or till puffed and golden. Rest it for 10 minutes. Good warm or cold.

YOU CAN
✱ omit cheese. Add nutmeg and a few herbs.
✱ make Asparagus Tart. Use 1 onion and a bunch of spring onions. Place 10 steamed/boiled spears asparagus in tart before adding cream mix. Bake.
✱ make Pizza Tart. Make tomato sauce (pg 106) with lots of garlic. Add 3 beaten eggs. Tip into cooked pastry. Top with olives, basil. Bake.
✱ make Leek Tart. Wash and slice 700g/1½lb leeks (white stems) into 2cm/1in chunks. Soften in 25g/1oz butter and 3 tbsps water for 5 minutes. Cool. Stir into cream mix above with extra Cheddar. Bake.

Cheat's Tomato Tart

Use all-butter puff pastry for health and best flavour.

1. Preheat oven to 200°C/400°F/gas 6. Grease a large baking tray.
2. Roll pastry out in a 30cm/12in circle using a plate for a template. Cut a 1cm/½in strip off the edge. Brush with water. Stick it back as a frame.
3. Place on baking tray. Prick with a fork. Spread thinly with sauce or passata. Arrange tomatoes in a single layer. Season. Scatter herbs, cheese.
4. Brush frame with egg wash. Bake 20 minutes, longer if needed, till base is crisp. Remove. Drizzle oil, herbs, salt.

YOU CAN
✳ make a 35x28cm/14x11in rectangular tart to feed more
✳ top passata with sliced griddled aubergine, grated cheese
✳ slice and fry button mushrooms in oil/butter. Lay over base. Scatter chopped garlic, fresh herbs.
✳ top with caramelized onion (pg 132)
✳ make baby tarts. Cut smaller pastry circles. Frame or cut an edge. Prick inner base. Top with **either** pesto, cherry tomatoes, goats cheese, oil, seasoning and basil, **or** mustard, mozzarella, sliced tomato, oil, salt and basil.

 FEEDS 2   EXPRESS

Half a 375g/13oz pack all-butter puff pastry
3 tbsps smooth tomato sauce (pg 106) or passata with 1 clove garlic, crushed
5–6 tomatoes, thinly sliced
Fresh basil or pinch dried/fresh thyme
A little freshly grated Parmesan/ Cheddar (optional)
1 egg for brushing
A little olive oil
Salt (preferably sea salt) and pepper

2 tbsps oil
2 onions, finely chopped
3 cloves garlic, crushed
1 stick celery, sliced
2–3 large carrots
1 potato, peeled, diced
450g/1lb leeks
1–2 tbsps plain flour
150ml apple juice
Splash of cider vinegar/white wine
    vinegar
425ml/15fl oz veg stock/Marigold
    bouillon
2 tsps soy sauce
1 × 400g/14oz can butterbeans (or
    dried, soaked, cooked)
1–2 tsps Dijon mustard
A little Vegemite
Squeeze lemon juice
Salt and pepper
Herbs (fresh/pinch dried)
1 pack all-butter flaky pastry
    (thawed)
A little beaten egg/milk to glaze
Poppy seeds (optional)

Flaky Bean Pie

A good hearty dish for feeding hungry masses – it's best made with big butterbeans.

1. Heat oil in a large pan. Lightly fry onions, garlic, till soft.

2. Add celery, carrots, potatoes, leeks. Lightly fry for 10 minutes.

3. Sprinkle flour into mix. Stir in apple juice, vinegar, stock, soy sauce. Increase heat. Boil 2 minutes. Reduce heat. Simmer gently for 20 minutes.

4. Add beans, mustard, Vegemite, lemon, seasoning. Simmer for 10 minutes.

5. Add herbs. Remove. Tip into pie dish. Cool slightly or chill.

6. Preheat oven to 200°C/400°F/gas 6. Roll pastry out thinly on floured board. Lift over and down onto dish on the rolling pin.

7. Press and pinch edges to seal to dish. Trim with a knife. Cut two slits in top to release steam. Brush with beaten egg/milk. Sprinkle seeds. Cook 30 minutes or till crisp and golden.

YOU CAN
* vary veg and beans or make it a mushroom and bean pie
* use shortcrust pastry (pg 178)
* use one-third stock/two-thirds cheese sauce (pg 110) for a creamy pie

Stew & Herb Dumplings

Classic comfort food – sweet veg, lovely rich tomato sauce and light dumplings. This one's addictive.

1. Gently fry onion, garlic in oil for 5 minutes till soft. Add carrots, celery, parsnips, swede, potatoes. Cover. Cook gently 5–10 minutes.
2. Add other ingredients. Boil. Reduce heat. Simmer, covered, for 20 minutes. Meantime, make dumplings.
3. Sift flour into bowl. Add butter. Rub together lightly (pg 10). Add herbs, cheese, egg. Mix to a sticky dough with a fork. Place large spoonfuls of mix onto simmering stew. Cover.
4. Cook 20–30 minutes until light and fluffy. Sprinkle fresh herbs.

YOU CAN:
✻ make Goulash: add 2 tsps paprika, caraway seeds at step 2. Add 2 tbsps yogurt/sour cream to finish.
✻ make Hotpot: cover with parboiled thinly sliced spuds. Bake in oven.
✻ reheat. Cover with grated cheese. Grill before eating.

2 tbsps oil
1 large onion, roughly chopped
2–3 fat cloves garlic, crushed
2 big carrots, sliced
3 sticks celery, finely sliced
2 parsnips, chunked
Bit of swede, chunked
500g/18oz potatoes, in chunks
1 x 400g/14oz can tomatoes
700ml/1¼ pints veg stock
2 tbsps tomato purée
1 tsp paprika
Loads of fresh parsley
Salt and pepper
Squeeze lemon juice

Dumplings

110g/4oz self-raising flour
50g/2oz butter
2 tbsps fresh/pinch dried herbs
A little grated cheese (optional)
Salt and pepper

151

FEEDS 2–3

VEGAN

4 large Savoy/spring cabbage leaves
1 x tomato sauce (pg 106) or
   mix passata with 1 clove garlic,
   crushed

Stuffing

1 small onion
2 fat cloves garlic
A little oil or butter
110g/4oz long-grain rice
300ml/10fl oz hot water/veg stock
A few mushrooms, diced
1 courgette, diced
Squeeze lemon juice
Salt and pepper
½ tsp mixed spice
A few raisins, pinenuts
A little grated cheese (optional)
Any fresh herb

Roast Stuffed Cabbage

Makes a great Sunday Roast … with a difference.

1. Drop leaves in boiling water 3 minutes to blanch. Remove.

2. Dunk in cold water. Drain. Dry. Set aside.

3. Stuffing: fry onion, garlic gently in oil/butter in saucepan till soft. Stir rice in. Add water/stock. Boil. Reduce heat to low. Cook 10 minutes or till just tender.

4. Lightly fry the mushrooms and courgette. Add to rice with remaining ingredients. Preheat oven to 190°C/375°F/gas 5.

5. Cut any hard stem from base of leaves. Place stuffing on each leaf. Fold into parcels. Spread a bit of tomato sauce into dish. Top with parcels, seams down. Cover or surround with sauce.

6. Cook, foil-covered, for 30 minutes. Remove foil. Cook for 20 minutes. Good served with sour cream and roasties (pg 162).

YOU CAN
✽ stuff with fresh or left-over risotto
✽ stuff with cooked brown rice (pg 12)/couscous (pg 133)/bulgur (pg 13)/ quinoa (pg 13), plus any diced vegetables, adding nuts and/or fried vermicelli

Thai Green Curry

Deep Thai flavours for such a quick dish.

FEEDS 2–3 VEGAN EXPRESS

1. Heat oil in a large pan. Cook onion, chilli, garlic gently for 2–3 minutes. Add curry paste. Cook, stirring for 2–3 minutes.

2. Add the aubergine. Cook for 4 minutes. Add sweet potato. Cook 2 minutes. Add stock and coconut milk.

3. Bring to the boil. Reduce. Simmer for 5 minutes. Add beans, mushrooms, lime leaves. Simmer for 5 minutes. Add the sugar, lime juice, seasoning. Eat with sticky or other rice (pg 12).

YOU CAN

* use chestnut mushrooms, add baby corn, tofu
* add grated ginger, lemongrass

1 tbsp oil
1 onion, finely chopped
½ mild red chilli, de-seeded, chopped
2 cloves garlic, crushed
1–2 tbsps good green curry paste
1 aubergine, quartered, sliced
1 sweet potato, peeled, chopped into chunks
225ml/8fl oz veg stock
340ml/12fl oz coconut milk
Fine green beans, halved
A few shiitake mushrooms, sliced
4 kaffir lime leaves
2 tsps brown sugar
Juice of 2 limes
Salt and pepper

Choice of:

2 sweet potatoes
2 old potatoes, peeled or handful
   new/salad potatoes
2 carrots
2 parsnips
Chunks of swede
2 red onions
2 cloves garlic, crushed
Beetroot, quartered
Whole garlic cloves
Chunks of lemon
Bay leaves/rosemary/thyme or
   sprinkle dried herbs
4 tbsps olive oil
Salt and pepper

Roast Root Vegetables

Transform regular root veg into something special.

1. Preheat oven to 200°C/400°F/gas 6. Peel all veg. Cut into chunks/wedges. Mix oil, crushed garlic, herbs (bash in pestle and mortar if you like).

2. Toss veg in herby oil with whole garlic and lemon chunks. Season. Roast in a baking tray for 30–40 minutes. Check progress every 10 minutes.

3. Meantime, cook rice (pg 12), couscous (pg 133), quinoa (pg 13) or pasta to accompany. Eat hot or cold with garlic yogurt herb dressing (pg 186).

YOU CAN

✳ roast aubergines, corn, courgettes, shallots, peppers, asparagus, squash
✳ eat on couscous, top with a poached egg or griddled halloumi

Ratatouille Gougère

A rich choux pastry with garlicky stewed Mediterranean vegetables.

1. Heat oil in large pan. Add onion, garlic. Fry gently till soft.

2. Add aubergine, courgettes, pepper. Fry gently 5–10 minutes.

3. Add cinnamon, tomatoes, pureé, sugar, lemon, seasoning. Boil briefly. Reduce heat. Simmer 30 minutes or till as soft as you like it. Add herbs. Taste and adjust seasoning.

4. Gougère: preheat oven to 200°C/400°F/gas 6. Sift flour, salt, mustard, cayenne onto greaseproof paper. Heat butter and water in pan. Boil. Remove. Shoot flour mix in, beating vigorously for 2 minutes to make a paste ball. Cool for 5 minutes.

5. Beat eggs in, bit by bit, along with the Cheddar/Gruyère till incorporated, for a smooth shiny paste. Make a 25cm/10in ring with tbsp blobs on a greased baking tray.

6. Cook 35 minutes or till high and golden. Fill with ratatouille.

YOU CAN

✱ use ratatouille as a side dish or layer into lasagne/cannelloni, fill pancakes. Pile onto baked potatoes, chuck into cooked pasta. Good cold with salad.

FEEDS 2–3 · VEGAN OPT.

Ratatouille

1–2 tbsps olive oil
1 large red/white onion, finely chopped
4 cloves garlic, chopped
1 large aubergine, chunked
2 courgettes, sliced
1 red pepper, de-seeded, sliced
Good pinch cinnamon
1 x 400g/14oz can tomatoes
1 tbsp tomato pureé
Pinch sugar
Chunk of lemon (optional)
Salt and pepper
Bit of fresh thyme/oregano

Gougère

100g/3½oz white bread flour
Pinch salt
Pinch mustard powder
Pinch cayenne powder
75g/3oz butter, diced
200ml/7fl oz cold water
3 eggs, beaten
3oz/75g strong Cheddar/ Gruyère, grated

FEEDS 4–6 **VEGAN OPT.**

1 medium onion, finely chopped
3 fat cloves garlic (2 crushed, 1 sliced)
3 tbsps olive oil
1 x 400g/14oz can chopped tomatoes
Pinch sugar
1 tbsp mushroom ketchup
A little chopped fresh coriander
6oz/175g chestnut/button mushrooms, roughly chopped
4oz/110g fresh white breadcrumbs (pg 12)
2oz/50g ground almonds
110g/4oz cooked peeled chestnuts, halved
Good pinch ground cinnamon
Small pinch dried thyme/sage
A good squeeze of lemon juice
1 egg
Salt and black pepper

Classic Nut Roast

Makes a good Christmas dinner any day of the week. Get chestnuts tinned or vac-packed.

1. Use first five ingredients to make tomato sauce (pg 106). Add ketchup and coriander. Tip into a large bowl to cool a bit.

2. Preheat oven to 180°C/350°F/gas 4. Lightly oil a 450g/1lb loaf tin. Line base with baking paper. Prepare remaining ingredients and mix into the tomato sauce.

3. Tip mix into the tin and level out. Cover loosely with foil. Bake for 50 minutes. Uncover. Cook for 10 minutes.

4. Run a knife round the edges to loosen. Invert onto plate. Slice.

YOU CAN

✳ vegans – substitute egg with 1–2 tbsps soy milk/tomato juice/Vegemite

✳ eat with roasties, veg (stir-fried cabbage), blitzed tomato sauce or onion gravy (pg 184). Great warm or cold with salads, tzatziki (pg 53), baked spuds (pg 60) couscous (pg 133), rice (pg 184), quinoa (pg 13).

✳ use roughly chopped walnuts, pecans, cashews, brazils

✳ save time – use left-over tomato sauce for tomato base

Asian Potato Cakes

Brilliant with stir-fry, salad or for dipping – make with fresh mash or left-overs.

1. Mix mash, mayo, garlic, chillies, soy sauce, coriander, seasoning with a fork.

2. Shape into cakes. Coat in flour/cornflour. Dip into beaten egg. Coat with breadcrumbs.

3. Heat oil in frying pan. Fry cakes gently, turning, till hot and crispy.

YOU CAN

✳ drizzle with chilli sauce

✳ add diced mushrooms fried with garlic

✳ sit the cakes on Asian Coleslaw. Grate 2 carrots, shred chunk white cabbage. Add finely chopped mint, grated ginger. Dress in ginger drizzle (pg 59). Top with seeds and crushed peanuts.

FEEDS 1–2   VEGAN   EXPRESS

1 bowl left-over or fresh, cooled mash
1 tbsp mayo
1 clove garlic, crushed
1–2 red chillies, de-seeded, diced
Splash soy sauce
Fresh coriander, chopped
1 egg, beaten
Flour/cornflour
Fresh/dried breadcrumbs (pg 12)
Vegetable/olive/sunflower oil

Potatoes Dauphinoise

Meltingly soft spuds in garlicky cream sauce – team with crisp green beans or side salads.

1. Preheat oven to 180°C/350°F/gas 4. Butter an oven dish.

2. Peel and slice potatoes as thinly as you can. Swirl in cold water.

3. Rinse and dry. Layer half in dish. Season with salt and pepper.

4. Mix cream, milk and garlic. Pour half over the potatoes.

5. Top with potatoes, more cream, dot with butter. Cover with foil.

6. Bake 1 hour. Remove foil. Bake another 30 minutes.

YOU CAN

✳ bake Cheese Potatoes. Simmer 300ml/10fl oz milk, 3 cloves chopped garlic, 450g/1lb thinly sliced potatoes, a thinly sliced onion for 10–15 minutes till just tender. Spoon into dish with grated Cheddar. Top with more cheese. Foil bake 30 minutes, or bake 30–40 minutes uncovered. Layer in other veg if you like.

FEEDS 2–3

Butter for greasing
900g/2lb floury potatoes (e.g. King Edward, Maris Piper)
Salt and pepper
300ml/10fl oz double cream plus bit of milk
6 cloves garlic, crushed

GREAT MASH & SIDE DISHES

Mix and match these with your main courses for awesome tastes, health and variety – vegetables should never taste boring.

Cauliflower Cheese

Feeds 4
  1 large cauliflower

Cheese sauce
  50g/2oz butter
  50g/2oz plain flour
  600ml/1 pint milk
  175g/6oz strong Cheddar
  1 tsp mustard
  Juice of ½ lemon
  Salt and pepper

Topping
  Extra Cheddar, grated

1. Cut and discard cauliflower leaves. Break head into florets.
2. Wash. Add to boiling water or steam in colander over pan. Cook 10 minutes then drain.
3. Meantime, make cheese sauce (pg 110).
4. Preheat oven to 230°C/450°F/gas 7 or preheat grill.
5. Put cauli into ovenproof dish. Cover with sauce. Add extra cheese.
6. Bake 30 minutes plus or grill till hot and bubbling.

YOU CAN
✳ cover with sliced tomatoes
✳ use broccoli instead
✳ add hard-boiled egg, spinach
✳ use steamed leeks

Buttered Leeks

Feeds 2
  2 medium leeks
  1 tbsp butter
  Salt and pepper

1. Discard dark green leaves.
2. Slit stems lengthways in half.
3. Wash under running water.
4. Slice across or cut in thin lengths.
5. Melt butter in pan. Add leeks, seasoning.
6. Cover with greaseproof paper.
7. Cook on low till very soft – about 10 minutes.

Stir-Fried Broccoli

Feeds 1–2
  2 tsps sesame oil
  1 tbsp sunflower oil
  2 cloves garlic, sliced
  A little fresh ginger, grated
  200g/7oz tenderstem or other broccoli
  4 tbsps water/stock
  2 splashes soy sauce
  2 tbsps veggie oyster/hoisin sauce

1. Heat wok or pan. Add oils. Heat.
2. Add garlic, ginger. Stir-fry a few seconds. Add broccoli. Toss and turn for 2–3 minutes.
3. Add water/stock. Reduce heat. Cover. Fry 2–3 minutes till softening but crisp. Add sauces.

YOU CAN
✳ stir-fry thinly shredded cabbage, in butter, garlic, soy sauce
✳ stir-fry green beans in garlic, sesame oil. Add cashews for last 2 minutes.

Carrot Pasta

Feeds 3–4
  4 carrots, peeled
  25g/1oz butter
  1 flat tbsp caster sugar
  Rind of ½ lemon
  Squeeze lemon juice
  Fresh parsley/thyme
  Salt and pepper

1. Cut carrots into ribbons with potato peeler.
2. Drop into boiling water for 20 seconds. Drain.
3. Melt butter and sugar in pan.
4. Add carrots. Stir-fry gently for 2–3 minutes till just soft.
5. Add rind, juice, herbs, seasoning.

YOU CAN
✳ cut carrots in sticks. Mix with butter, orange/lemon juice. Add herbs. Season. Cook in foil parcels at 200°C/400°F/gas 6 for 30 minutes.

Green Beans & Tomato

Feeds 2–3
  200g/7oz fine beans
  A little olive oil
  2 cloves garlic, diced
  1 tomato, chopped small
  Salt and pepper

1. Put beans in pan. Cover with boiling water from a kettle.
2. Boil 5 minutes/till just softening. Drain.
3. Heat oil in a pan. Add garlic. After a few seconds, add tomato, then beans, seasoning. Turn till hot.

Red Cabbage

Feeds 4
  1 red cabbage, finely sliced
  1 onion, roughly chopped
  1 large apple, roughly chopped
  1–2 cloves garlic, sliced
  3 pinches mixed spice/
    cinnamon
  Salt and pepper
  1 tbsp brown sugar
  1–2 tbsps wine vinegar
  A few dabs of butter

1. Preheat oven to 180°C/350°F/gas 4.
2. Layer veg and apple in dish.
3. Sprinkle garlic, spice, seasoning, sugar between. Pour vinegar in. Dot with butter. Cover.
4. Bake 30–40 minutes, stirring once. Taste. Adjust balance of flavourings.

Cumin Cauliflower

Feeds 2–3
  1 cauliflower, in small florets
  3 cloves garlic, peeled, sliced
  Olive oil
  1 tsp ground cumin
  Salt

1. Preheat oven 220°C/425°F/gas 7.
2. Tip cauli, garlic onto baking tray.
3. Drizzle a bit of oil, sprinkle cumin, salt. Turn to coat. Roast till tender (about 20 minutes).

YOU CAN
***** add broccoli florets

Chillied Chickpeas

Feeds 4

225g/8oz dried chickpeas
Pinch bicarbonate of soda
1 large onion, finely chopped
3 cloves garlic, crushed
110ml/4fl oz olive oil
3 red chillies, de-seeded, finely
  chopped
1 tsp cumin powder or 2 tsps
  cumin seeds
110ml/3½fl oz passata
Salt
Fresh coriander, torn

1. Cover chickpeas with triple
volume water.
2. Add bicarb, leave to soak overnight.
3. Drain. Boil 2–3 hours or till tender.
4. Fry onion and garlic in oil over low
heat till soft.

5. Add chillies, cumin. Cook 3
minutes.
6. Add chickpeas, passata, salt,
coriander.
7. Simmer for 20 minutes.

YOU CAN

* add chopped, de-seeded tomato
* top with spinach and yogurt
* add chopped red onion, avocado
* use tinned chickpeas

Corn on the Cob

Feeds 2

2 corn cobs, whole
1 tbsp butter
1 chilli, de-seeded, chopped
Lime or lemon juice

1. Remove leaves from corn. Wash.
2. Drop cobs into boiling water.

3. Cook 5 minutes. Drain.
4. Put into foil with butter, chilli, juice.
5. Wrap into parcels. Bake at
200°C/400°F/gas 6 for 20 minutes
until tender.

YOU CAN

* barbecue slowly for 20 minutes
* add honey, mustard to butter
* boil for 20–30 minutes

Hot Tomatoes

Feeds 2

3 tomatoes, halved
1–2 cloves garlic, crushed
Salt
Pinch sugar
Olive oil
Basil leaves (optional)

1. Preheat oven to 230°C/450°F/gas 8.
2. Spread tomato halves with garlic,
salt, sugar, oil, optional leaf.
3. Roast 10–15 minutes.

YOU CAN

* top with pesto (pg 187)

Butternut Squash

Feeds 2

1 butternut squash
2 cloves garlic, sliced
Knob of butter
Lemon juice
Olive oil
Salt and pepper

1. Preheat oven to 230°C/450°F/gas 6.
2. Cut squash in half lengthways with
a sharp knife on flat surface.
3. Scoop seeds and fibre out with
a spoon. Scatter garlic, butter,
juice.

4. Brush surface with oil. Bake on tray 40 minutes or till tender.

YOU CAN

✳ spoon flesh out. Mash with 3 handfuls grated cheese, grated ginger, honey, seasoning. Replace in shell. Bake 20 minutes.

✳ cut raw squash into wedges. Griddle or barbecue, turning once.

Mix & Match Green Salad

Feeds 2

> Any green leaves (e.g. salad lettuce, iceberg, cos, little gem, rocket, watercress, whole chicory, spinach, pea shoots)
> Olive oil
> Wine vinegar

1. Use or mix any leaves.

2. Dress: **either** toss in olive oil and wine vinegar at the table, **or** mix dressing of choice (pg 185–187) and combine in a bowl using your fingers for maximum coating. Serve.

Onion Salad

Feeds 2

> 1 onion, peeled
> A length of cucumber, peeled
> 2 pinches dried mint
> 1 tsp sugar
> Pinch cayenne powder
> Lemon juice
> Salt

1. Slice onion v thinly. Separate rings.

2. Tip into a bowl with everything else except salt. Taste.

3. Add salt prior to serving.

YOU CAN

✳ replace cucumber with 2 very thinly sliced, de-seeded tomatoes

Asparagus

Feeds 2

> Fresh asparagus spears
> Squeeze lemon juice
> Butter
> Mayonnaise/Hollandaise sauce

1. Heat a frying pan of lightly salted water.

2. Bend each spear to see where woody end stops. Cut away. Add spears to boiling water.

3. Boil 4 minutes plus, till crisply tender. Test with a knife. Serve with lemon, melted butter, mayo/ Hollandaise sauce.

YOU CAN

✳ chargrill it – oil, turn on griddle

✳ toss in salad dressing

✳ sprinkle garlic breadcrumbs (pg 103)

✳ dip into soft-boiled eggs

Crunchy Onion Rings

Feeds 1–2

> 1 onion, peeled
> Milk
> White flour
> Salt and pepper
> Vegetable/sunflower oil

1. Slice onion horizontally and separate into thin rings.

2. Tip into a dish. Cover with milk.

3. Sprinkle flour/seasoning on a plate.

4. Pour oil into wok/pan at least 8cm/3½in deep.

5. Heat till a breadcrumb crisps (180°C/350°F).

6. Dip onion into flour. Fry till crisp.

Vitamin Boost Citrus Salad

Feeds 2

> 2 oranges, peeled, sliced, chopped
> A few fresh/dried dates, chopped
> 2 carrots, peeled, grated
> Green leaves of choice
> Nuts and seeds of choice
> Honey Mustard or other dressing (pg 187)

1. Prep fruit, carrots, leaves, nuts, seeds, dressing.

2. Mix, toss, serve.

YOU CAN

✳ use grapefruit and avocado. Sit on toasted ciabatta.

Baby Potatoes

Feeds 2

350g/12oz baby new potatoes
A little salt
Butter (plain or herby)
Squeeze lemon juice

1. Boil kettle.
2. Put washed spuds in pan with salt and cover with boiling water. Boil 10–15 minutes till soft.
3. Drain. Top with butter, salt, squeeze lemon.

YOU CAN

* crush spuds with a fork. Drizzle olive oil, salt.
* roll spuds in butter, garlic, loads of chopped parsley
* cook, slice. Grill in a dish with grated cheese, spring onion, sour cream, herbs, mustard.

Frying-Pan Crunchy Potatoes

Feeds 2

4 large floury potatoes or
left-over boiled potatoes,
chopped into bite-size chunks
Oil for frying
Salt and pepper
A few springs thyme
Lemon juice

1. Boil spuds until just tender, drain well. Or chop left-overs.
2. Heat oil in a large pan. Add cold or freshly cooked potatoes. Fry very slowly for 20 minutes, turning regularly till crisp.
3. Sprinkle seasoning, thyme, juice.

YOU CAN

* add a few chopped shallots
* make Patatas Bravas. Top with smooth tomato sauce (pg 106) with additional chilli. Add a fried whole chilli and garlic mayo.

Garlic & Herb Nibbles

Feeds 2–3

4 large floury potatoes
Olive or vegetable oil
6–8 cloves garlic, chopped
3–4 sprigs rosemary/thyme
Bit of sea salt

1. Preheat oven to 230°C/450°F/gas 7.
2. Dice potatoes into v small cubes and dry with clean tea towel.
3. Mix with oil, garlic, herbs, salt.
4. Bake in roasting/baking tin in a single layer for 40 minutes/till crunchy.

Roasties

Feeds 2–3

4 large floury potatoes, peeled
Olive oil
Salt and pepper

1. Boil potatoes for 10 minutes or till almost tender.
2. Drain well. Halve or quarter them.
3. Preheat oven to 230°C/450°F/gas 6. Tip oil into tin. Put into oven to heat for 2 minutes.
4. Add potatoes. Turn to coat. Season.
5. Roast 30 minutes plus, till crispy. Season.

YOU CAN

* roast in well-scrubbed skins
* roast whole unpeeled waxy/baby potatoes
* coat in curry paste, lemon, garlic before roasting
* add rosemary/sage/garlic cloves
* roast peeled sweet potatoes
* roast halved carrots, parsnips

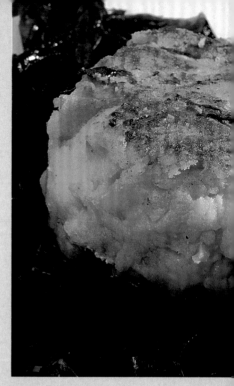

Creamy Mash

Feeds 2

450g/1lb old floury potatoes,
(e.g. Maris Piper, Rooster,
King Edward)
Pinch salt
75ml/2½fl oz milk
50g/2oz butter
Salt and pepper

Optional flavourers
Garlic, crushed
Dijon/English mustard
Lemon juice
Grated nutmeg

Fresh dill, parsley, coriander, basil, chopped

1. Peel and quarter potatoes. Add to pan of boiling water with a pinch of salt. Cook, with lid on, 15 minutes or until tender.
2. Drain well. Tip back into warm pan. Shuffle pan over low heat 30 seconds. Add hot milk. Mash with a fork or masher.
3. Add butter, seasoning, optional flavourers. Season to taste. Beat with a wooden spoon.

Sweet Potato Mash

Feeds 2
    450g/1lb sweet potato, peeled, cut into large chunks
    A few gratings fresh ginger
    Butter

1 tsp honey
Squeeze lemon/lime
Salt and pepper

1. Boil potato with ginger.
2. Drain. Tip back into pan. Shuffle over heat.
3. Mash with butter, honey, lemon/lime, seasoning.

Irish Champ

Feeds 2
    450g/1lb old floury potatoes
    2 cloves garlic
    100ml/3½fl oz milk
    3 spring onions, finely chopped
    A little chopped fresh parsley
    50g/2oz butter
    Salt and pepper

1. Cook whole potatoes, garlic in boiling water for 20 minutes/till tender.
2. Heat milk gently with spring onion, herb for 4 minutes. Set aside.
3. Drain spuds, saving garlic. Return to pan on heat. Shake 1 minute. Remove. Hold in tea towel. Peel. Tip back into pan with two-thirds butter, garlic. Mash well.
4. Beat in warm milk, spring onions, seasoning till creamy. Serve in bowls with butter.

YOU CAN
✱ top with a poached egg

French Cheese Mash

Feeds 2
1. Cook potatoes as above with 2 cloves peeled garlic.

2. Drain. Dry. Peel. Mash with butter, 2 tbsps milk.
3. Beat in 110g/4oz Gruyère/Cheddar over heat.
4. Add two sliced spring onions, seasoning.

Bubble & Squeak Cake

Feeds 1–2
    1 bowl left-over/fresh cooled mash
    ½ bowl left-over/fresh cooled cooked cabbage (to cook it, shred then boil 2–3 minutes)
    Bit of beaten egg
    Salt and pepper
    White flour/cornflour
    Olive oil or oil and butter

1. Mix mash, cabbage, egg, seasoning.
2. Flour your hands. Shape mix into burger-style cakes.
3. Tip flour onto a plate with more seasoning. Coat cakes in mix.
4. Fry in hot oil on medium/low heat, turning once till crisp outside, piping hot in the centre.

YOU CAN
✱ make veg potato cakes with diced cooked veg instead of cabbage
✱ make Cheesy Potato Cakes. Use grated Cheddar, smoked paprika, grated onion, herb.
✱ make Greek Potato Cakes with crumbled feta, diced black olives, thyme. Eat with tzatziki (pg 53).
✱ make plain potato cakes to have on the side or as the main event with eggs, mushrooms, beans, salsa, salsa verde (pg 185), veg, salad

PUDDINGS

 PER PERSON **VEGAN**

1 nectarine/peach
2 plums/apricots
1 banana, peeled, cut into 5cm/2in
   lengths
Lemon juice
4–6 strawberries
3–4 tbsps apple/orange juice
Caster sugar
Ground cinnamon

Grilled Fruit Skewers

Heating up your fruit brings out the sweetness.

1. Using wooden skewers? Soak them in cold water for 20 minutes.

2. Brush banana with lemon juice. Halve and stone nectarine or peach, plums or apricots.

3. Marinate all fruit in orange/apple juice for 20 minutes.

4. Preheat grill/barbie. Line grill pan with foil. Sprinkle sugar, cinnamon on a plate. Thread fruit onto skewers.

5. Turn fruit in sugar mix. Grill 3 minutes. Turn. Cook till just browning. Drizzle marinade. Sprinkle more mix. Eat with yogurt (pg 18) honey, nuts and ice-cream.

YOU CAN
✳ make Fresh Fruit Kebabs. Drizzle chocolate/raspberry sauce (pg 183).
✳ bake in a parcel. Chop fruit. Sit on foil/greaseproof paper. Drizzle with juice and sprinkle cinnamon. Fold and seal parcel. Bake on tray for 10 minutes at 220°C/425°F/gas 7.
✳ serve in parcels

Toffee Bananas

Fast five star fruit pudding – don't burn the caramel.

25g/1oz butter
3–4 bananas, peeled
1½ tbsps sugar
A good splash orange juice
Squeeze lemon juice

1. Melt butter in frying pan. Add whole bananas. Fry gently for 3 minutes or till browning. Turn. Fry for 2 minutes.

2. Add sugar to pan. Stir to melt till it browns without burning.

3. Turn fruit again to coat with liquid toffee. Add orange/lemon juices.

YOU CAN

✱ pile on toasted brioche, eat with ice-cream

✱ bake 4 halved bananas in foil-covered dish with 200ml/7fl oz orange juice, 1 tbsp brown sugar, 1 tbsp lemon juice, innards of 1 passion fruit, 25g/1oz butter at 180°C/350°F/gas 4 for 20 minutes.

Baked Peaches

Effortless chic. Roasting peaches enhances the flavour.

2 peaches, halved
Orange/apple juice
2 tbsps lemon juice
1–2 tsps brown sugar
A little butter
4 raspberries

1. Sit peaches in a greased dish. Drizzle with juices to cover base.

2. Top each half with butter, sugar and a raspberry. Bake for 20–30 minutes at 180°C/350°F/gas 4 till hot, tender, bubbling.

YOU CAN

✱ stuff with crushed amaretti, butter, sugar, egg yolk

FEEDS 2 · EXPRESS

1–2 bananas, peeled, chopped
1–2 apples, peeled, chopped

Batter
50g/2oz plain white flour
Pinch fine salt
1 tsp icing sugar
2 tsps butter, melted
4 tbsps warm water
1 egg white
Sunflower oil for frying

Sprinkle
Caster sugar
Cinnamon

Hot Apple & Banana Doughnuts

A great snack or finger-food pudding – try dunking in my chocolate or fresh raspberry sauces (pg 183).

1. Sift flour, salt, icing sugar into a bowl. In another bowl, mix butter and water.

2. Beat or whisk this into flour/sugar mix till smooth. Whisk egg white until stiff. Fold into batter with metal spoon (pg 10). Add fruit, turning.

3. Heat 9cm/3½in oil in a deep pan/wok till a breadcrumb crisps. Fry doughnuts 2–3 minutes or till crisp, brown turning once.

4. Sit on kitchen roll. Roll in sprinkles. Eat immediately.

Jam Soufflé Omelette

Light as a soufflé without all the effort.

1. Melt jam in a pan with water. Set aside. Preheat grill to medium.
2. Whisk egg whites till stiff (pg 11). Beat or whisk yolks, sugar, milk in a second bowl till mix thickens. Fold egg whites in gently (pg 10).
3. Heat butter in a 15cm/6in frying pan. When it froths, slide the mix in. Cook gently for 1–2 minutes till the base just sets. Sit pan under a medium grill for 1–2 minutes till risen but soft. Slide onto plate. Drizzle melted jam. Fold. Sprinkle icing sugar.

YOU CAN

∗ make Sharing Omelette. Whisk 3 large egg yolks, grated rind and juice of 1 lemon, bashed cardamom seeds. Add stiffly whisked whites. Cook as above. Drizzle jam/lemon curd. Eat from pan at the table.

∗ drizzle with warm blueberry compôte (pg 27) or apples fried in butter and sugar or runny honey, nuts and chopped bananas

FEEDS 1   EXPRESS

1–2 tbsps any jam
A little water

Omelette
2 large eggs, separated
1 tsp caster sugar
1 tbsp milk
A little butter

Icing sugar

Rhubarb Mess & Popping Candy

Soft, sharp fruit, crunchy meringue, creamy base and a taste explosion.

1. Mix sugar, honey, hot water to dissolve. Add cordial and juice.

2. Preheat oven to 200°C/400°F/gas 6. Tip liquid into tin/dish with rhubarb. Roast 5 minutes till rhubarb's soft, holding shape. Lift intact from liquid. Set aside.

3. Boil liquid for 2–3 minutes to reduce to a syrup. Set aside.

4. Sit a berry in each glass. Layer rhubarb, lightly whipped cream, crumbled meringue, syrup and repeat. Put popping candy in meringue layers. Top with cream, candy, rhubarb, drizzle syrup.

FEEDS 3–4

2 tsps brown sugar
2 tsps honey
125ml/4fl oz hot water
3 tsps elderflower cordial
3 tsps lemon juice
5 sticks rhubarb, 4cm/1½in lengths
Fresh raspberries/blackberries
300ml/10fl oz double/whipping cream
3–4 meringues, bought or homemade (pg 79)
1 pack popping candy

YOU CAN
* make Eton Mess. Sit chopped strawberries in orange juice with a bit of icing sugar. Chill. Whisk cream softly. Stir in berry mix and crumbled meringue. Maybe add raspberries. Or use mango/passion fruit.

Brandy Snap Baskets

Get a bit creative moulding your biscuit.

MAKES 6–8   VEGAN OPT.

50g/2oz granulated sugar
50g/2oz butter
2 tbsps golden syrup
2 tsps lemon juice
50g/2oz plain white flour
1 level tsp ground ginger

1. Heat sugar, butter, syrup gently. Stir to dissolve. Add lemon juice. Remove from heat.

2. Add flour and ginger. Mix till smooth. Cool 10–15 minutes.

3. Preheat oven to 180°C/350°F/gas 4. Grease two non-stick trays. Put tablespoonfuls of mixture well apart on trays (it spreads dramatically).

4. Bake 8 minutes till lacy, golden. Check after 5 minutes as they burn fast. Remove from oven.

5. Cool 1–2 minutes. Lift off with a spatula while warm. Press to mould on upturned jars/bottles while still warm.

6. Cool. Fill with cream/berries.

YOU CAN
* fill with ice-cream, sliced banana/berries, chocolate/butterscotch sauce
* fill with chilled lemon mousse (pg 182)
* leave snaps flat or make cones. Use to sandwich/hold ice-cream.
* roll round wooden spoon handle for curls. Cool. Dip into chocolate.

175g/6oz stoned dates (fresh or
    dried) chopped
300ml/10fl oz water
1 tsp bicarbonate of soda
50g/2oz butter
175g/6oz sugar
2 eggs, beaten
175g/6oz self-raising flour
1 tsp vanilla extract

Sauce
25g/1oz butter
2 tbsps golden syrup
175g/6oz soft brown sugar
4 tsps single cream

Sticky Toffee Pudding
Old school pudding classic – everyone loves this.

1. Preheat oven to 180°C/350°F/gas 4. Grease a 28x18x2.5cm/
11x7x1in baking tin.

2. Simmer dates, water in a pan for 5 minutes. Add bicarb. Set
aside.

3. Cream butter, sugar with a wooden spoon/beater for 3 minutes
or till light and creamy. Drizzle egg in gradually, beating hard. If
mixture curdles, beat in a pinch of flour.

4. Stir in sifted flour, date mix, vanilla. Spoon into tin. Cook 30
minutes or till risen, springy. Cut into squares. Keep warm.

5. Sauce: melt butter, syrup, sugar in pan over low heat. Boil 1
minute. Stir in cream. Pour over pudding immediately.

YOU CAN
* eat cold as cake, use in trifle, reheat with sauce/custard
* substitute a bit of water with cold coffee
* add a few crumbled walnuts

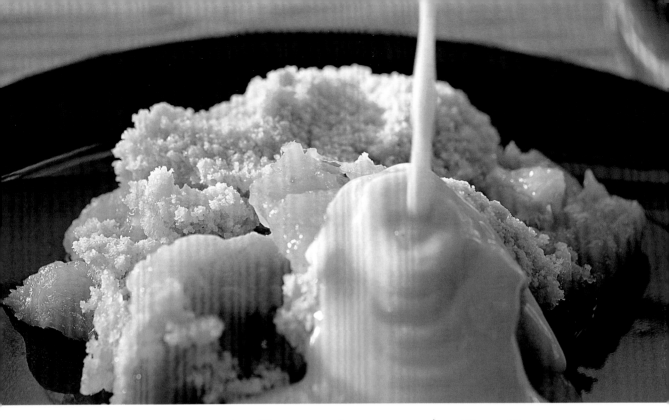

Mango Crumble & Custard

A tropical take on a great British pudding.

1. Preheat oven to 180°C/350°F/gas 4. Peel and slice mangoes and banana. Arrange in ovenproof dish with sugar, cinnamon.
2. Sift flour, salt into a bowl. Rub butter in (pg 10). Add sugar. Sprinkle lightly over fruit. Cook 20–30 minutes. Eat with custard (pg 187) or ice-cream.

YOU CAN

✱ add lime juice, pineapple, passion fruit
✱ add cinnamon, mixed spice, grated lemon, ground almonds to crumble
✱ make Apple Crumble. Stew 3 peeled, sliced, cored apples in 2 tbsps water, 1 tbsp sugar, 2 tsps butter on low heat for 5 minutes. Use as above. Cook 30–40 minutes. Vary with banana, raspberries, poached plums (pg 37).
✱ make rhubarb crumble. Poach 500g/17oz rhubarb in 4 tbsps water, 1 tbsp sugar for 3–4 minutes. Tip into dish. Add raw strawberries if you like. Top with crumble.

2 large mangoes
1 banana
Sprinkling of brown sugar
2 pinches cinnamon

Crumble
175g/6oz white flour
Pinch salt
75g/3oz butter
75g/3oz caster sugar

MAKES 4 **EXPRESS**

60g/2¼ oz good dark chocolate,
   broken into squares
60g/2¼ oz soft butter
½ tsp orange rind
2 tsps cold black coffee
2 medium eggs
2 extra egg yolks
50g/2oz caster sugar
50g/2oz plain flour, sifted

Little Hot Chocolate Puddings

It's all in the timing for an oozy centre – don't overcook them.
If the worst happens, whip up a chocolate sauce (pg 183).

1. Put a baking tray into the oven. Preheat oven to 180°C/350°F/
gas **4.** Grease four 150ml/5fl oz ramekins/dishes.
2. Tip chocolate, butter, rind, coffee into a bowl. Sit it over a pan
of simmering water (pg 12). Leave it to melt slowly. Remove, then
stir together. Set aside.
3. Whisk eggs and sugar together for 4 minutes till pale, mousse-
like, doubled in volume. Add chocolate mix and flour. Fold in lightly
using a large metal spoon (pg 10). Divide between ramekins. Place
on the hot tray.
4. Bake in ramekins on a tray for 10–12 minutes (don't open
door) till risen and firm outside, saucy inside (test with toothpick).
Eat from dish, or loosen sides with a knife and invert onto plates.

Baked Cheesecake

My favourite cheesecake – I've not found a better one.

FEEDS
6

1. Grease a 23cm/9in loose-bottomed circular cake tin. Bash biscuits to crumbs in a freezer bag using a rolling pin. Melt butter and stir into crumbs. Mix. Press into tin. Chill 15 minutes. Preheat oven to 150°C/300°F/gas 2.

2. Beat remaining ingredients to a smooth mix or blitz with a processor/handblender. Tip onto chilled base. Bake 35–40 minutes. Turn heat off.

3. Leave to cool in oven for 1 hour. Remove. Cool and chill for 2 hours.

4. Leave plain or top with whipped cream, berries.

225g/8oz digestive biscuits
75g/3oz butter
700g/1½lb curd/cream or
  Philadelphia cheese
175g/6oz caster sugar
3 eggs
2 tbsps sour cream
Juice and rind of ½ lemon
A few drops vanilla extract

YOU CAN
∗ make classic Banoffee Pie. Boil an unopened 400g/14oz can condensed milk in a pan of water for 4 hours (top up water in pan). Cool. Open. Spread on chilled biscuit base. Top with sliced bananas, whipped cream, grated chocolate.

1 x pancake batter (pg 34)

Filling
200ml/7fl oz whipping or double
   cream
1 tbsp caster sugar
2 tsps ground ginger
225g/8oz fresh raspberries
Maple syrup and lemon juice for
   drizzling
Icing sugar for dusting

Raspberry Ginger Cream Pancakes

Decadent…

1. Make pancake batter (pg 34).

2. Make filling: tip cream into a bowl. Whisk until it just holds shape. Stir in the sugar and ginger. Add raspberries.

3. Cook pancakes (pg 34). Lay on warm plates. Pile filling onto one corner of each pancake.

4. Fold pancakes in half and half again. Drizzle syrup and lemon juice. Sprinkle dusting of icing sugar.

YOU CAN FILL WITH

✳ sliced bananas, cream and butterscotch sauce (pg 183)

✳ mixed berries, ice-cream and chocolate sauce (pg 183)

✳ chopped apples fried in butter, sugar and lemon

Toffee Lemon Fruit Cups

Cheat's crème brûlée. Tastier, healthier…

MAKES 4

EXPRESS

1. Place fruit in cups to two-thirds full.

2. Whip cream softly. Fold in lemon curd. Spoon into cups till just below rims. Chill for 20 minutes or till needed.

3. Spoon sugar into a heavy-bottomed pan. Let it melt over gentle heat until golden (no darker). Pour a layer over each cup. It sets in 2 minutes.

Choice of fruit
Bananas, sliced
Fresh berries
Mango chunks soaked in lime juice

200ml/7fl oz double/whipping cream
2 tbsps lemon curd (pg 187)
110g/4oz caster sugar

YOU CAN

✳ make Toffee Apples. Stick lolly sticks into 8 apples. Heat 450g/1lb sugar, 3 tbsps golden syrup, 150ml/5fl oz water in a deep pan on low heat. Stir. Boil without stirring till toffee is golden red/brown (170°C/325°F). Remove. Dunk apples to coat. Set on buttered greaseproof/baking paper.

Lemon Tart

Chic French classic. Check the pastry's cooked before adding the filling.

1. Sift flour, salt into a bowl. Add butter. Rub in (pg 10). Add water. Mix to a stiff non-sticky dough with a fork. Roll lightly to a smooth ball. Chill 30 minutes, film-wrapped. Preheat oven to 190°C/375°F/gas 5.

2. Roll on a lightly floured board to fit and line a greased 20.5cm/8in tart tin (pg 11). Prick base lightly. Bake, lined with greaseproof paper weighed down with dried/baking beans, for 15–20 minutes. Remove paper and beans. Cool.

3. Sit a large bowl over a pan of gently simmering water (base not touching). Add lemon rind, juice, eggs, sugar, butter. Melt slowly, stirring constantly till it's thick enough to coat the back of a wooden spoon (10–15 mins). Cool 5 minutes. Tip into tart base. Cool. Chill for 2 hours.

4. Sprinkle icing sugar. Serve at once or flash under hot grill to glaze.

FEEDS
6

110g/4oz plain white flour
Pinch salt
50g/2oz butter, diced
1–2 tbsps very cold water

Filling
Rind and juice of 6 lemons
6 eggs, beaten
175g/6oz caster sugar
25g/1oz butter

Sprinkling of icing sugar

YOU CAN

✱ make Lemon Meringue Pie. Use juice and rind of 2 large lemons, 3 large eggs, 175g/6oz caster sugar, 225g/8oz butter to make curd as above. Tip into cooked base. Make meringue with 110g/4oz caster sugar, 2 egg whites. Spread over tart. Bake 10–15 minutes at 150°C/300°F/gas 2.

✱ make Treacle Tart. Mix 9 tbsps breadcrumbs, 9 tbsps golden syrup, 1 tbsp lemon juice, grated rind, 3 tbsps cream. Tip into pricked uncooked pastry case. Bake 25–30 minutes at 190°C/375°F/gas 5.

✱ make Cheat's French Apple Tart. Roll ½ pack puff pastry into a rectangle (pg 11). Slice 3 cored crisp apples very thinly. Douse in lemon juice, melted butter, 3 drops vanilla. Layer onto pastry in overlapping rows. Sprinkle with caster sugar. Bake 15 minutes at 200°/400°F/gas 6. Brush with a little melted apricot jam if you like.

Yorkshire Apple Dumplings

Your own apple pie … perfect with custard.

MAKES 4

VEGAN OPT.

1. Make pastry and chill (pg 178). Preheat oven to 220°C/325°F/ gas 7.

2. Peel apples. Core them to two-thirds down. Divide sugar, dates, rind/cinnamon between the 4 cavities. Brush with lemon juice.

3. Divide pastry into 4. Roll into 4 circles large enough to enclose apples. Sit apples in centre. Brush pastry edges with water, then draw up to cover, pinching to seal at the top. Mould to neaten. Sit on greased tray. Cut out pastry leaves with spare pastry. Make a slit in the top. Brush with egg wash. Bake 10 minutes. Reduce heat to 180°/350°F/ gas 4 for further 30 minutes. Remove. Sprinkle caster sugar. Eat with custard (pg 187), ice-cream, yogurt (pg 18).

Pastry
225g/8oz plain flour
110g/4oz butter
Pinch salt
1–2 tbsps cold water

Filling
4 medium apples
40g/1½oz sugar
2 dates
Lemon rind or cinnamon
Milk/beaten egg for brushing

YOU CAN

✱ make Apple Pie. Make pastry with 350g/12oz flour and 175g/6oz butter, 3 tbsps water. Use ⅔ to line a brownie-style tin 30.5x18x3cm/11x7x1¼in. Fill with 900g/2lb thinly sliced apples, 2 tbsps sugar, cinnamon, grated lemon. Top with remaining pastry. Make slits, brush with milk. Cook as above till golden, filling tender.

✱ vegans – make incision around middle of unpeeled, cored apples. Stuff. Bake in a little orange juice for 40 minutes.

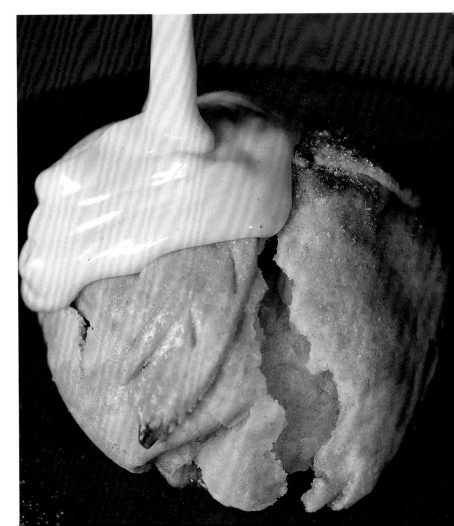

FEEDS
4

Soft butter
400g/14oz brioche loaf or stale
  bread
2 bananas or 150g/5oz dried fruit
Cinnamon
Juice of ½ lemon
Granulated sugar/3 tbsps melted
  marmalade

Custard
4 large eggs
225ml/8fl oz cream
450ml/16fl oz milk
A few drops vanilla extract
150g/5oz caster sugar

Bread & Butter Pudding

Make it special with brioche or transform your stale bread.

1. Butter a shallow pie dish. Cut the bread/brioche into 12 slices. Butter thickly. Cut across diagonally.

2. Lay half the slices, butter side down, over the base of the dish. Add sliced banana/dried fruit, sprinkle with cinnamon and a little lemon juice. Cover with remaining slices, butter side up.

3. Beat together custard ingredients. Sieve then pour over pudding. Leave to soak for an hour or two (or overnight).

4. Preheat oven to 180°C/350°F/gas 4. Sprinkle sugar over pud. Bake for 50 minutes or until top is golden. Or brush with melted marmalade 10 minutes before end of cooking.

YOU CAN
✳ use French bread, pain au chocolat, stale tea cakes
✳ layer in sliced peach, mango, plum, lightly poached rhubarb (pg 173), apple
✳ spread first layer of buttered bread/brioche thickly with lemon curd (pg 187)/apricot jam/marmalade, or add 110g chocolate chunks
✳ make it savoury. Spread buttered bread with garlicky tomato sauce. Add grated Cheddar, herbs, seasoning to a sugar-free custard.
✳ tuck in sliced tomatoes, mozzarella, dried oregano, fresh basil, cayenne

Summer Pudding

Classic use for stale bread – it's packed with berries. Use frozen out of season or try apples, blackberries, plums, cranberries.

FEEDS 4   VEGAN

110g/4oz caster sugar
2 tbsps orange juice
2 tbsps lemon juice
150ml/5fl oz orange juice
900g/2lb mixed soft red fruit
   (raspberries, strawberries,
   blackcurrants, redcurrants)
2–3 fresh mint leaves (optional)
6–8 slices good white bread
Extra fruit to decorate

1. Heat sugar and juices in a medium pan, stirring until sugar dissolves. Boil 2–3 minutes till syrupy. Add two-thirds fruit (and mint leaves, if using) for 1 minute to release juices. Remove from heat to cool a little. Add remaining fruit.

2. Line a 1.2-litre/2-pint pudding bowl with two-thirds of the bread slices. Fit/tear to cover completely. Spoon fruit into the lining, saving a bit of juice to pour over the pudding later.

3. Use last of the bread to make a lid to cover and seal the bowl. Sit a plate and weights on top. Chill a few hours or overnight.

4. Run a knife around the edges. Invert onto a plate. Shake out. Pour extra juice over. Eat with cream, ice-cream.

YOU CAN
* make solo puds in ramekins/cereal bowls
* add softly poached rhubarb
* bake Plum Toasts. Spread 4 large slices bread with soft butter creamed with cinnamon. Cover base of a dish. Stuff 8 halved, stoned plums with brown sugar. Place, cut side down, on bread. Dot extra butter, sugar. Bake 20 minutes at 190°C/375°F/gas 5.

MOUSSES, ICE-CREAM & SAUCES

Here are some of my favourites for a decadent finish – enjoy.

Chocolate Mousse

An all time favourite.

- **175g/6oz good dark or milk chocolate, broken into chunks**
- **2 tbsps cold strong black coffee or water**
- **1 level tbsp butter**
- **1 tbsp orange juice**
- **Pinch salt**
- **4 large eggs, separated (pg 11)**

1. Put chocolate, cold coffee/water, butter into a heatproof bowl. Sit over a pan of barely simmering water (pg 12). Leave to melt slowly. Stir till smooth. Remove. Leave to cool. Beat in the orange juice then egg yolks till glossy.

2. Whisk egg whites and salt until stiff. Fold lightly into chocolate mix with a large metal spoon (pg 10). Don't overwork. Spoon into cups or dishes. Chill for 2 hours or longer.

Lemon Mousse

Creamy yet sharp – have it in a glass or pile it on trifle.

- **300ml double cream**
- **½ tsp vanilla extract**
- **Juice of 2 medium lemons (and zest of 1)**
- **25g icing sugar, sifted**
- **1–2 tbsps apple juice**

1. Pour cream into a large cold bowl. Add the vanilla extract and lemon zest.

2. Whisk gently with a balloon whisk, gradually adding the juices and sugar for a soft cream that forms peaks. Taste and adjust.

3. Pour into glasses/cups and chill.

YOU CAN

✳ stir in whole raspberries, passion fruit pulp, well mashed banana

Lemon Yogurt Ice-Cream

- **Juice and rind of 3–4 lemons**
- **175g/6oz icing sugar, sifted**
- **250ml/9fl oz Greek yogurt**

200ml/7fl oz double cream
3 tbsps very cold water

1. Mix lemon juice and rind in a bowl.
2. Stir in sifted icing sugar gradually.
3. Leave 30 minutes to infuse flavours.
4. Whip yogurt, cream, water till softly thick. Add the lemon/sugar mix.

5. Freeze in freezer box/bag. Remove 10 minutes before serving.

Peach Sundae

6 peaches
1 tbsp sugar
2 tbsps lemon juice
1 sprig rosemary (optional)
1 x raspberry sauce (below)
1 x good vanilla or own lemon ice-cream

1. Cover peaches with water in pan. Add sugar, juice, rosemary. Boil for 1 minute. Simmer for 4. Remove from the liquid. Cool.
2. Make raspberry sauce (see below). Peel skins off peaches.
3. Slice peaches. Layer into glasses with ice-cream. Add raspberry sauce.

YOU CAN
✱ vary fruit. Use chocolate or butterscotch sauce.

Fresh Raspberry Sauce

225g/8oz raspberries
1 tbsp icing/caster sugar

1. Heat berries and sugar in pan till soft, releasing juice.

2. Press through a sieve over a bowl. Eat or chill.

Best Chocolate Sauce

110g/4oz dark chocolate
15g/½oz butter
2 tbsps water
2 tbsps golden syrup
1 tsp natural vanilla extract

1. Put everything except vanilla into a bowl.
2. Sit it over a pan of simmering water (pg 12).
3. Let it melt, then stir till smooth. Add vanilla.

YOU CAN
✱ store in fridge for 1 week

Butterscotch Sauce

25g/1oz butter
2 tbsps golden syrup
175g/6oz soft brown sugar
4 tbsps single cream

1. Melt butter, syrup, sugar in pan.
2. Boil briefly, then stir in cream.
3. Use on ice-cream, bananas, pancakes.

Mars Bar Sauce

1 Mars bar, chopped
3 tbsps milk

1. Stir Mars bar and milk in a pan until almost melted (leave bits of caramel).
2. Pour immediately over ice-cream.

ESSENTIAL EXTRAS

These essentials make all the difference – no veggie menu's complete without them.

Onion Gravy

Knob of butter or 1 tbsp oil
1 large red or white onion, v
    thinly sliced
1 fat clove garlic
Pinch sugar
Pinch salt
4 chestnut/button mushrooms
Pinch dried thyme
Splash mushroom ketchup
300ml/½ pint veg stock or
    water
1 tsp redcurrant jelly
Lemon juice
Black pepper

1. Heat butter or oil in a pan. Add onions, garlic, salt, sugar. Cook gently on low heat 10–15 minutes or till soft and golden. Stir occasionally. Add mushrooms, thyme. Cook 4 minutes.
2. Add mushroom ketchup, stock or water. Boil for 1 minute. Reduce heat to simmer for 5–10 minutes. Add redcurrant jelly, lemon juice. Season.

Own Ketchup

500g/18oz ripe tomatoes,
    quartered (stalks and stems
    attached)
2 cloves garlic, crushed
50g/2oz brown sugar
60ml/2½oz cider vinegar/white
    wine vinegar
Pinch mustard powder
4 shakes Henderson's Relish/
    Tabasco

1. Boil everything up in pan.
2. Reduce heat and simmer gently 45–60 minutes or till thick.
3. Remove stalks, stems. Blitz till smooth. Sieve. Cool.
4. Pour into sterilized jars (see Apple Chutney, below). Seal. Cool. Store chilled.

YOU CAN

* add one medium onion, quartered, and fresh chilli

Vegetable Stock

2 large onions
1 celery stick
2 leeks
3 carrots
A few black peppercorns
Fresh parsley sprigs
2.3 litres/4 pints water
2 garlic cloves
1 bay leaf
Lemon juice and rind (optional)
1–2 tsps salt

1. Wash and roughly chop all veg.
2. Tip into a large pan with other ingredients. Boil. Reduce heat.
3. Simmer, half covered, for 1–2 hours (minimum 30 minutes) till reduced by a third. Strain through colander.
4. Refrigerate for a week or freeze.

YOU CAN

* fry veg gently in oil/butter for 10 minutes at step 1
* add well-scrubbed veggie peelings, lemon rind
* add a few mushrooms, vary herbs
* boil to reduce by half. Freeze in ice-cube trays. Reconstitute with boiling water.

Apple Chutney

2kg/4½lb cooking apples,
    peeled, cored, chopped
4 cloves garlic, crushed
600ml/1 pint malt vinegar
700g/1½lb soft dark brown
    sugar
125g/4½oz stoned dates,
    chopped
3 tsps ground ginger
1 tsp ground mixed spice
Large pinch cayenne pepper
1 tsp salt

1. Tip apples, garlic, half the vinegar into a large heavy-based pan.
2. Cook gently, stirring regularly, till thick and sludgy.
3. Add remaining ingredients. Cook gently for 30 minutes. Stir and check for sticking.
4. Wash and dry jars. Sterilize in oven at 140°C/275°F/gas 1 for 10 minutes. When chutney is thick, soft but not too smooth, ladle into warm jars. Place a wax disc from a jam kit directly onto chutney. Dampen a cellophane disc to cover each pot.
6. Secure with an elastic band. Wipe jars while warm. Leave 2 months before eating.

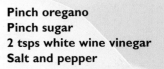

Cucumber Pickle

1 fat cucumber, peeled, very thinly sliced
1–2 small white onions, very thinly sliced
1 tbsp chopped dill
175g/6oz sugar
1 tsp salt
125ml/4fl oz pint white wine vinegar

1. Mix cucumber, onions, dill.
2. Pour mix of sugar, salt, vinegar over.
3. Tip into clean sterilized jar or airtight container.
4. Chill. Eat next day. Store 2 weeks.

Mango Chutney

1–2 mangos, peeled, diced

Small red onion, peeled, diced
1 red chilli, de-seeded, chopped
1 tbsp lime or lemon juice
1 tsp caster sugar
Fresh coriander leaves, chopped
Salt and pepper

1. Chuck everything into a bowl. Add seasoning.
2. Taste. Adjust flavourings if you need to.

Re-Fried Beans

1 medium onion, finely chopped
1 clove garlic, crushed
1 tbsp olive oil
1 x 400g/14oz can red kidney beans/150g/5oz dry beans, cooked (pg 12)
Pinch cumin

Pinch oregano
Pinch sugar
2 tsps white wine vinegar
Salt and pepper

1. Fry onion and garlic in oil till soft.
2. Add rinsed beans, spices. Fry till mushy, mashing a bit.
3. Add vinegar to taste, season.

Salsa Verde

1 bunch parsley
1 bunch basil
3 cloves garlic
1½ tbsps capers
1 tbsp Dijon mustard
1 tbsp white wine vinegar
6–8 tbsps olive oil

1. **Either**: blitz everything in processor or blender. **Or**: chop herbs, garlic, capers finely by hand, then stir in mustard, vinegar, oil.
2. Taste. Adjust. Store in fridge, covered.

Blue Cheese Dressing

4 tbsps olive oil
½ tsp runny honey
½ tsp Dijon mustard
Juice of ½ lemon
Up to 50g/2oz blue cheese

1. Mix first four ingredients.
2. Mash cheese in.

Oriental Dressing

75ml/3fl oz sunflower oil
1 tsp sesame oil
4½ tsps white wine vinegar
1 tbsp soy sauce
1 clove garlic, chopped (optional)

Whisk the lot together.

Yogurt Dressing

250g/9oz Greek yogurt
1 tsp lemon juice
1 tsp honey
1 tsp wine vinegar
1 tsp mustard
1–2 tbsps chopped dill/other herb
Salt and pepper

Mix everything together.

Mayo

2 egg yolks
½ tsp salt
½ tsp dry mustard
½ tsp caster sugar
250ml/9fl oz sunflower/
   groundnut oil
50ml/2fl oz olive oil

2 tsp white wine/cider vinegar
   or lemon juice
1 tbsp hot water

1. Sit bowl on tea towel. Add yolks, salt, mustard, sugar. Beat with balloon whisk/wooden spoon.
2. Mix oils in jug. Add to eggs, drip by drip, beating constantly. Don't rush or it will curdle.
3. Add 1 tbsp vinegar/juice when half oil's in and mayo's thickening. Add oil in slow stream, beating.
4. Add rest of vinegar/juice and water. Taste. Adjust.

YOU CAN

✱ add 2 crushed cloves garlic
✱ add 2 tsps harissa, horseradish, mustard
✱ beat in an egg yolk if it curdles

Pesto

25g/1oz pinenuts
110g/4oz fresh basil, chopped
2 cloves garlic
½ tsp salt
150ml/5fl oz olive oil
50g/2 oz grated Parmesan

1. Toast nuts 1–2 minutes in dry pan.
2. By machine: blitz basil, nuts, garlic, salt in processor. Add oil gradually. Stir in Parmesan.
3. By hand: bash garlic, salt, in pestle & mortar. Mash in other ingredients, stirring cheese in at end.

YOU CAN

✱ store in fridge for a week
✱ stir into hot new potatoes, mash, baked spuds, tomato soup, rice and pasta salads. Stir into hot trofie

pasta for a pasta-to-go box.

* spread on savory tarts, into sarnies, toasties

Salad Dressing

1 tsp English/Dijon mustard
1 tsp caster sugar
1 clove garlic (optional)
1½–2 tbsps wine vinegar (red, white, cider, sherry)
6 tbsps olive oil
½ shallot (optional)
Chopped parsley (optional)
Salt and black pepper

Either: shake everything together in a jar for a thick emulsion.

Or: mix all except oil in a bowl. Whisk that in to finish.

YOU CAN

* add to leaves in bowl. Toss with your fingers.
* toss dressed leaves with fork and spoon at table
* drizzle it

Honey Mustard Dressing

2 tsps mustard of choice
1 tsp honey, caster sugar
1 clove garlic, crushed
2 tbsps wine vinegar/lemon juice
6 tbsps olive oil
Salt and black pepper

Either: shake everything in a jar till emulsified.

Or: whisk everything except oil in a bowl, then add oil.

YOU CAN

* use 1½ tbsps balsamic vinegar
* add a finely chopped shallot

DIY Cream Cheese

600ml/1 pint DIY natural yogurt (pg 18)/bought Greek yogurt
1 tsp salt

1. Line a sieve/colander with a bit of muslin.
2. Sit it into the top of a bowl.
3. Stir salt into yogurt. Tip into muslin.
4. Leave to drip 6 hours/overnight till cheese forms.
5. Eat as is with sweet or savoury extras. Good for cooking. Store in fridge 1 week.

Garlic Bread

1 French stick/baguette
Lots of soft butter
2–3 cloves garlic, crushed
Fresh herbs (optional)
Lemon juice (optional)

1. Preheat oven to 200°C/440°F/gas 6.
2. Beat butter, garlic, extras together.
3. Slash bread diagonally, leaving slices intact at the base.
4. Spread butter into cuts. Foil wrap. Bake 25 minutes.

Cheat's Raspberry Jam

250g/9oz raspberries
250g/9oz caster sugar

1. Preheat oven to 180°C/350°F/gas 4. Wash jar. Dry in oven.
2. Lay fruit in shallow dish. Bake 20 minutes.
3. Stir sugar in. Spoon into jar. Seal. Cool. Store in fridge.

Custard

300ml/10fl oz milk
A few drops vanilla extract/vanilla pod, split, seeds exposed
3 egg yolks
10g/½oz caster sugar
5g/¼oz cornflour

1. Heat milk gently with extract or pod. Remove just before it boils. Remove pod.
2. Beat egg yolks, sugar, cornflour in bowl.
3. Stir milk in slowly using a wooden spoon.
4. Return to pan, stirring on very low heat till it thickens – don't let it boil. Curdling? Sit pan in cold water and beat hard.

YOU CAN

* use in Bread & Butter Pudding (pg 180), trifle
* add sliced banana

Lemon Curd

Juice and grated rind of 2 big unwaxed lemons (or 3 small)
110g/4oz caster sugar
50g/2oz butter
2 large eggs, beaten

1. Sit a bowl into a pan of gently simmering water (base clearing).
2. Add lemon juice and rind, sugar, butter. Melt very slowly.
3. Add egg. Stir constantly over very low heat until thickening to coat the back of a spoon. Cool. Store in a jar/bowl in the fridge.

Index

A big **thank you** to all these lovely people for being there for me and always supporting me – Mum, Dad, Tom, Polly, KR, Alice, Louise, Henry P, Joe, Andy, Dom, Jamie, Ferg, Elwess, Penty, Sophie, Emily, Jordan, Tom Y, Felicity.

First published 2010 by Walker Books Ltd
87 Vauxhall Walk, London SE11 5HJ

10 9 8 7 6 5 4 3 2 1

© 2010 Sam and Susan Stern

Photography by Jeffrey Stern
Additional photographs by Lorne Campbell (70b, 83, 174, 177) and Peter Goulding (168).
The right of Sam Stern and Susan Stern to be identified as authors of this work has been asserted by them in accordance with the Copyright, Designs and Patents Act 1988

This book has been typeset in GillSans. Printed in China.

British Library Cataloguing in Publication Data: a catalogue record for this book is available from the British Library
ISBN 978-1-4063-1975-0
www.walker.co.uk   www.samstern.co.uk